WHISPERS FROM HEAVEN

WHISPERS FROM HEAVEN

REX ELSASS

ethos
collective

WHISPERS FROM HEAVEN © 2024 by Rex Elsass. All rights reserved.

Printed in the United States of America

Published by Igniting Souls
PO Box 43, Powell, OH 43065
IgnitingSouls.com

This book contains material protected under international and federal copyright laws and treaties. Any unauthorized reprint or use of this material is prohibited. No part of this book may be reproduced or transmitted in any form or by any means, electronic or mechanical, including photocopying, recording, or by any information storage and retrieval system, without express written permission from the author.

LCCN: 2024917420
Paperback ISBN: 978-1-63680-350-0
Hardcover ISBN: 978-1-63680-351-7
e-book ISBN: 978-1-63680-352-4

Available in paperback, hardcover, e-book, and audiobook.

All Scripture quotations, unless otherwise indicated, are taken from the Holy Bible, New International Version®, NIV®. Copyright © 1973, 1978, 1984 by Biblica, Inc.™ Used by permission of Zondervan. All rights reserved worldwide.

Scripture quotations from The ESV® Bible (The Holy Bible, English Standard Version®) are notated with ESV. © 2001 by Crossway, a publishing ministry of Good News Publishers. Used by permission. All rights reserved.

Any Internet addresses (websites, blogs, etc.) and telephone numbers printed in this book are offered as a resource. They are not intended in any way to be or imply an endorsement by Igniting Souls, nor does Igniting Souls vouch for the content of these sites and numbers for the life of this book.

Some names and identifying details may have been changed to protect the privacy of individuals.

Dedicated to Reid

Table of Contents

Foreword ix
Introduction xiii

January: God's Love 1
February: Praise 33
March: Brotherly Love 63
April: God's Beautiful Creation 97
May: Surrender 131
June: Gratitude 169
July: Unity 201
August: Peace 233
September: Child of God 265
October: God's Presence 299
November: The Gift of Life 333
December: Trust 365
About REID Foundation 397

Foreword

I randomly met Rex Elsass at an Italian restaurant in Dublin, Ohio. It was a chance encounter, but we have been circling each other in our professional careers for years. We have been on opposite sides of many tough political battles in our years in Ohio politics, him as a Republican and me as a Democrat. Yet, we came to understand that we have a common mission: To heal those who suffer from trauma and addiction.

Rex came to this issue through his son's struggles with addiction and then his heartbreaking death a few years ago. It was an unimaginable nightmare for any parent, and Rex, understandably, carries that pain with him every day. Rex now spends a great deal of his time trying to bring forth real solutions to reduce the pain and suffering that so many Americans deal with.

I developed a passion for this work during my 20 years in Congress working with Veterans returning from war with Post Traumatic Stress and many Ohioans struggling, overdosing, and dying from addiction. These tragedies left much trauma behind with families, loved ones, and the broader community and country. These events hang over all of us like a dark cloud that will not go away.

Later, Rex and I got together for a long and joyful lunch. We laughed, we teared up, and we talked about how we can move the country towards healing the trauma and addiction we see ravaging our country.

After that lunch, Rex started to share with me by text message his daily prayers that he wrote first thing every morning. I was so inspired by his ability to write about God in a way that penetrated deep into my soul. I could feel his words. He moved me toward gratitude and an increased awareness of God's immense presence in our lives moment to moment. Along with my other spiritual texts I read every morning, his prayers got my mind aligned with my soul at the beginning of each day.

It wasn't long before I started to rely on his morning prayers. The prayers felt like a bright shaft of light breaking through those dark clouds. And, so, I audaciously told my new friend that he should publish these prayers for other parents in his situation.

Not knowing the depth of pain he feels or others who have tragically lost loved ones too early in their lives, I could still see how his words would be able to comfort others so they feel they are not alone in their suffering. I could see these prayers helping others to ground themselves in God, our Creator, Divine Providence, or whatever other way we view our ultimate reality.

And for some reason, my heart told me to tell him that if he did publish these I, as a lifelong Democrat, would write the foreword for him, a lifelong Republican. He took me up on my offer, and I'm glad he did.

If Rex and I, after lifelong campaigns and arguments, can join together to recognize God's work and blessings in our daily lives, no matter the pain, then all Americans can, too. If we start our day with God at the center, then we will see God working in our lives and in our fellow citizens, and that perspective will change our lives and our country. That worldview will unleash God's grace to flow through us so we can heal others while we are simultaneously being healed.

That is the power of prayer. And this book is one small but mighty step in the direction of a more compassionate and God-centered country. My hope is that these prayers will unleash His Spirit through you as we, together, make our country and world a more gentle, forgiving, and Godly place.

Tim Ryan
Member of Congress
2003-2023

Introduction

Shortly after Reid transcended to Heaven, I was inspired to write these daily prayers with little of my own effort, and I feel they are inspired by him. For the last several years, I've shared them with friends and people I have met who I felt would benefit from this encouragement. It has become a part of my daily devotion and meditation practices.

After much encouragement, I have chosen to share them more broadly through this book to benefit the REID (Reaching Everyone In Distress) Foundation, which I founded four years ago.

Our nonprofit organization is dedicated to utilizing the healing power of music and creative expression to bring "front-line therapy" and prevention to communities and those impacted by the opioid crisis, substance abuse, mental health issues, or life crises. We have served thousands of people in Ohio prisons, rehabs, and many other weekly sites to bring healing through trained music therapists. Music brought Reid great peace and meaning in his life.

Introduction

We have also actively engaged in supporting public policy nationally to promote research for the healing of trauma through emerging therapies. Most specifically, Ibogaine, which revolves around opioid withdrawal syndrome within 48 to 72 hours when properly administered in a clinically controlled medical setting. It appears to have the singularly unique ability to clear and reset the brain's opioid receptors while also restoring the brain's organic dopamine and serotonin production to pre-opioid exposure levels—a process that otherwise would not begin to occur until a person has been completely abstinent from opioid use for at least 18 months. This could bring unprecedented healing to the 100,000 dying each year of overdose.

Every book sold will assist us with the REID Foundation's efforts to bring unprecedented healing and hope to the world.

It is my sincere hope that this book will bring encouragement and blessing to each reader as I have been by these Whispers from Heaven.

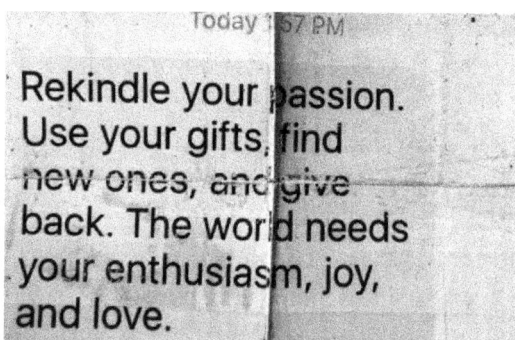

When I was going through a challenging time a decade ago, Reid sent me this text. I feel like he is still sending me encouragement by inspiring these whispers!

JANUARY: GOD'S LOVE

January 1

Hey Lord, it's me, Rex here! My son whispers to me from Your circle of serenity in Heaven. I receive and believe the Love of God in every word, allowing me to feel I'm with You above. I will delight in this day, feeling it is yet another way to be bold with Your expression of love. You gave me this day of life, for I am Heaven sent. So today, I'll fight to be Your light. I have come to know that I am here to grow. So the only thing I must do is shine this light You entrusted me with.

I've learned to love You by loving You in me. This love doesn't make me separate or unique. It's in true unity that our collective light shines, overcoming fright and worldly blight. Its mental bind dissolves when I'm simply kind. For we are each a piece of You. So the more individual pieces find unity, the closer we become to the collection through connection of Your reflection.

Amen.

January 2

May I have faith in impossibility. May I not be a serial quitter but a survivor with my eyes upon You.

I strive to give up trying on my own as I've grown in You. Open my heart and life to acceptance to simply allow Your story to unfold and mold me.

A friend recently shared some wisdom, "A leash is for animals," so I now know anyone who has walked alongside my journey of healing is free to go on their own at any time. I'm blessed by the time and journey together—even if only for a short time. Loving is letting go of everything and everyone to grasp onto God alone for my complete and unique healing in His presence.

Because I am Yours, You've promised me, "There is no condemnation." Then forgive me in each incident I have not extended Your peace, understanding, and deep love to ALL others as they are equally Yours.

I make mistakes, but I'm not a mistake. Roses have thorns that adorn the beauty of the flower. I can sing while enduring the thunderstorms. You see the beauty even through my struggle as You have planned it to end Heavenly.

Amen!

_____
_____
_____
_____
_____

January 3

I am loved by You . . . I know this to be true.

You have told me this in Your word that You left for me to read. You are the original masterpiece, and I am made in Your image to be like You. So I'm no mistake, for my soul is only Yours to take. I'm here to develop spiritual eyes so I can grow from any challenge. In this, I can recognize the light that will lead me to know You.

In time enough . . .

Grief and despair will disappear in Heaven's thin air. Until then, I'll live awakened with Your love flowing through me to all around me. Everyone I meet is the same reflection of You. So may You feel my love for You through the reverse flow from my brothers, sisters, and neighbors to You, the original creator from Your created. Within others, I see the miracle of You, this gift You have given so we can know You better.

As I am passing through this earth to come home to You, I am fully learning and delighting in this glimpse into the love that is awaiting us in eternal life.

Your light dissolves my misery and fear with Your kindness and goodness.

May the desires of my spirit overtake the needs of my ego, allowing grace and forgiveness to be first.

Amen!

_____
_____
_____
_____

January 4

You have chosen me to carry Your love. The world can be as cold as stone, but I am not alone. You have given me a megaphone glued to my heart from the start. I had to discover the hole within me in the dark valley where it was bleak and I freaked. I believed there was no spark.

But that is where I surrendered and finally put my survival trust in thee, for You alone are holy and gave me the spark in the dark valley and spoke to me lovingly. In my pain, I thought there was a permanent stain. But that is where You showed me how to drain my pain. It was only in my polarized fright that Your Godly might could communicate to me in a tongue I could comprehend. I now know the darkest night and my blight were essential for my saving purpose in Your brightest light.

So it was from Your saving love that You walked me through the valley. In it, I could not comprehend it. I could not even pretend!

Now it's Your love that reminds me of just who YOU are and who I am to YOU . . . YOUR BELOVED!

Amen.

January 5

I am God's light of love in this world. My dream is to have that love be contagious as God uses me to wipe away tears and bring laughter.

My value does not need to be proved, forged, or created as it arrived upon my first breath.

God's gift of security melts my doubt, allowing me to live in His trust and hope. So, as this day unfolds, it's with growing clarity that my life's foundations are built on my reality of God's love, protection, and care and knowing that He is always there.

When I forget this security, my soul awakens and reminds me.

God, I trust You as I must. You're always here.

Amen.

January 6

God, You are a loving presence, and You use me as Your expression. This undoubtedly makes me enough! I am loved by You, and I bathe in that love. You are who and what I am as I am Your presence of love. I have been worthy from the moment You conceived of my consciousness. Love is all there is. I am Your being of love illuminating this world. Your work in this world is through me. I am a blessing to the planet and to Your creation as I'm Your created. Joy is my divine right. The night recharges Your light.

I have enough, as Your blessings are limitless. My spirit remains in Your presence, and worldly news cannot minimize or confuse as You use me perfectly. No worldly chaos interferes with Your grace in this place.

Amen.

January 7

Take from me confusion and doubt. After all, what is that about? When I concentrate on Your love, compassion, and kindness, everything becomes simple. Grace is in this place in every space. Then the complication of my mind minimizes, and my heart expands as it understands and pours out Your love and kindness. I just need to feel and be Your love that flows through me. Your healing energy washes away doubt, for Your wholeness allows me to embrace You. Your goodness is the source of the blood running through my body. You dissolve my judgment for harmony. As I choose Your love, all that threatens me vanishes. Anything that is less than this melts away when I know and feel Your presence. Everything is in Your will and causes me to be free of sadness.

I am a child of God, which places a smile on my face and ends the worldly chase with no disgrace. I am awake, whole, and completely anchored in You!

Amen.

January 8

I'm learning to love myself through all that life has given me. I have to love myself as You made me to be, not as the world thinks I am. Those who surround me are from You to call me out from the fall from human misery to the Heavenlies. So the question is: Do I love You? Do I trust You? Could I recognize it's been You all along? I thought I was not enough, but now I know this is the deceit of defeat. You are the author of my victory!

I'm clearing my thoughts, bringing me astounding height in Your light. It stretches my ability to see You in both my tragedies and triumphs.

When I thought I was broken or not enough, You cheered me on from Heaven—that's my ultimate might instead of that bitter old fright.

I am Yours. I'm perfectly held in Your hand. I don't need any human to save me as my soul was healed by Your scars. I have no need of other opinions, worldly evaluations of my life, or assessments of my love.

Sin was vanquished as I stand before the throne of life. There is no death, only Your perfect love from my first breath.

Man's minimization and distortion of Your endless love will never hold me back. So I sing hallelujah, for there is only beauty in store. Not because I've earned it but because You gave it to me. This is the reason You created me: to experience and not have to earn Your love!

Amen.

_____

_____

_____

January 9

I am the light of the world. As a beacon on top of a mountain, I cannot be hidden, nor can this beacon within me be stifled. I release every unworthy part of me to be Your expression of love. I'm here to radiate the glow of this Godly flow as I grow in You. A child of Yours is healed within and is forevermore. You have proclaimed that I am missing all the blame in this game of Heavenly fame.

I surrender into Your arms daily to be reminded and renewed, as I am a unique expression of You. I just need to be reminded of whose I AM. As I stand in His light, I am healed, releasing all the sin inside of me. The sun shines on me, drawing me into God's loving family. God's love emanates through me, renewing daily.

Amen.

_____
_____
_____
_____
_____
_____
_____
_____
_____
_____

January 10

I am sheltered in Your love. Music blasts in my heart. Your energy vibrates my very being. I seek Your face as my creator. Why do I let fears of man separate us? You have never turned away from me; You reach me every day in every way. My soul sings Your hymns, and my spirit defies my human doubts. The land of the living causes me to gain understanding.

But I wait upon You, Lord, to instill continuous whispers of Your great love in me. The chants that defy what I know are silenced to shouts of joy as You are gracious to me. Cast out all my doubts the moment a fear rears its head. Give me an unquestioned understanding of Your perfect love. I wait patiently for You. I give thanks to You, especially when tension and doubt come about.

You are greater than any fear. The light of Your love extinguishes the darkness of anxiety. When it comes back to haunt me, all I need to do is remember who You are and not doubt Your light of love.

I sit upon the rock on the high ground. Here, Lord, I seek Your face in this worldly place. I lay down my mistakes to allow my heart to fully receive You.

Amen.

January 11

May I be tenderhearted and forgiving of others just as You have forgiven me. Tears fall down the wall of my heart, shedding guilt and shame. It is not for me to seek false fame, for that's all an earthly game. Your eternal heart is revealed when the wall blocking my heart falls. You perfectly designed me from the start; this is what I'm made for.

I can transcend all that has bothered me by existing from my soul. Those things that caused me to doubt were created by confusion. They were just passing emotions that come and go, but Your spirit is here with no end. Your permanent love designs my fate to be eternal life.

I concentrate on the eternal truth that bails me out. Why have I struggled when it's simple to accept the joy from an open heart and receive Your love?

All that is required of me is to surrender what was never meant to be and make room for Your love!

Amen.

_____
_____
_____
_____
_____
_____
_____
_____
_____

January 12

Lord of mercy, Lord of grace—with Your love, please fill this space.

In times of confusion, I look to You and remember that love comes from You. It seems I am never through with the trials that come my way, but then You renew my strength just when I need it.

Your love never ceases nor light ever dulls; it's always within. This constant truth of peace is always available to me, keeping me steady and sustained. Your love and strength are mine to stand on, and when I fall, You are there to land on.

I can always see Your unconditional love for me, after all.

Amen.

January 13

May I see, feel, and know the true depth of Your love for me as soon as I awake.

In this reality, I am free of all that burdens me. Instead of fear, I am instilled with Your love from above.

Any thought that is lesser than what You intended for me vanishes in Your clarity. With all You are and all You have done for me, Your love cannot be stifled or minimized, no doubt cast on the vastness of Your love. Your majesty is always bestowing limitless love from on high.

Transform my inner spirit to soar willingly on the shores of Your majesty, fueled by Your love in all grace and free-flowing mercy.

Amen!

January 14

One size fits all is not God's thing at all.

In the age to come, I will see that loving Him with all I've got and living to love in the here and now will be my greatest reward. You love me uniquely, in a way perfect for me. Beyond this age, Heaven holds all the love there could ever be, and I will wait for Your harvest to fulfill Your promise, eternity with You.

Amen!

January 15

Nothing can separate me from Your love, for it covers me. God, You are love, and You make me whole within. All my struggles bring me closer to You again.

Love, hope, and faith, the greatest of even these is love. You loved me first. Your constant love is my protection under the shadow of Your wings.

When I doubt this truth, everything comes apart at the seams. But my dreams restore me as they awaken this core truth in me. I, a child of God, am filled with Your love, the light that drives me to delight. Love overcomes fear, as God's banner of love calls us. Those who Love know God, for God is love! You delight in me with singing. I am more than a conqueror through His enduring love. Because God loves me, I can love others.

Amen!

January 16

Your steadfast love never departs from me.

Your promise is my transformation. When I believe and receive, Your peace is all I need. I realize it never was up to me; You paved the road for me to walk. I rest and am no longer in a worldly test. I look up and know that my soul within is Your truest kin, far from sin. For You are my spirit's glue to hold together all that is true.

Amen!

January 17

God, Your love is gracious and extravagant. It transforms my worries into the comfort of Your provision. Your sustaining love feeds me while your love teaches me to rest, trust, and receive willingly.

You gain my full attention when I am in my greatest need. You plant the seeds that grow me closer to knowing that You alone are creator, sustainer, friend, and savior. Your love is not because You want to gain anything from me but simply to give me everything. The warmth of Your presence waits for me.

The more I age, the less I see of me as I gain real understanding of Your fullness and grace.

In perceived difficulty, I learn true trust in thee. Now I can beam with this gleam in my heart that was there from the start. When I was a baby, I knew only pure love and trust, and I will be like this again when I eventually flee this land. That's because I was always to be in Your band with thee forever, made totally free by Your bond of love. It's greater than any gold, so I can be bold with the eternal light of Your love.

Amen.

January 18

God's love is poured out in me. As I look up and raise my arms high, I feel Your energy.

The light within is from my friend who created eternity. It frees me to be all that I was meant to be. I rest and cease the lease on my mind and simply surrender it to You for the sublime. That is when I'm fine, and it becomes natural to rhyme.

In time, I feel the blight diminished in Your light as I sit in Your delight. When I merely empty the land mines of thought, I myself create in my heart a new start by letting go and breathing. The calm within is now trading trouble for sustaining peace.

My heart grows as my mind slows. Negative emotions still and rest with my Father's heart to create serenity. This is my foretaste of Heaven when I'm united with the delight beyond all earthly insight.

Amen!

January 19

"God is love." His is not a sentimental, emotional kind of love but the love of the Father, who is the origin of all life, the love of the Son who dies on the Cross and is raised, the love of the Spirit who renews human beings and the world. Thinking that God is love does me so much good; it teaches me to love, to give myself to others as He gave Himself to me. He walks with me on the road through life, so I must love just as He loves me.

May I rise beyond passing emotion and feelings of being wronged. May I see the wounds of another and comprehend my own healing by bringing a healing in them and me.

As I am reminded, I am in a Heavenly state as You have made me first rate.

Amen!

_____
_____
_____
_____
_____
_____
_____
_____
_____
_____
_____

January 20

The LORD blesses me and keeps me; the LORD makes His face to shine upon me and is always gracious to me; the LORD lifts me up and gives me His very own peace, as you say in Numbers 6:24-26.

May I have the courage from this assurance to be all the insurance I need to let go of that which I cannot change, and may it cause me to rearrange. I am free to fully access my heart by simply releasing all of that which falsely prevents me from raising my energy. Then I no longer traverse to and fro but fly to Heavenly heights.

The human nature of God and the divine nature of man make it impossible to not trust as I must to end the rust. In life, I wear many hats, but You see through them. I no longer have many masks, for I only have one meaningful task. My heart glows with the face You grace upon me naturally.

If I am perfected in my Lord's love, fear has been cast from me as it's a suffering that would not last through Heaven's blast.

There is no fear in love as love casts out fear, which I thought I could not bare. But as I'm aware of this light, my uncertainty takes flight.

Peace is my surround sound, as it's where my heart is found.

Amen.

_____
_____
_____
_____

January 21

May my pursuit of truth always have love as its constant companion! May my thought and emotion be grounded in my love of You and in a genuine love and compassion for my neighbor. For God so loved the world, for God so loves me, His unfailing love pumps blood in my veins, which enables me to see THEE in His humanity.

I will find His energy in all I see and do unless my physical ego blocks the free flow within me. When I recognize it, I can easily tear down this wall without hesitation. I don't need the fake crown the world tries to give me, as I'm no earthly clown playing the fool.

So now I knit the part I know, a better fit with a Heavenly flow, the bit I've finally come to know. As I have been instructed in 1 Corinthians 13, Love does not need to have its own way. I have a full-time job of simplification as all my mind's complications prevented me from simply being the good Samaritan You sent me here to be. I bent the rules until I learned to trust, rested, and no longer tested. I'm guided by those who have transcended above, teaching me to live here with a Heavenly foretaste.

Amen!

_____
_____
_____
_____
_____
_____
_____

January 22

My mind can receive You because I truly believe and am at rest in my heart from this day's fresh start. No one can pluck me from the love of my Father's hand in this land. I am his, and I know right from creation's start that my very heart is made in the creator's likeness. I feel it and know it, so I can be it!

I don't need to raise my hand or walk to any stage. It's my countenance that says with certainty, "I am made by God, and I will one day return from where I've come." I suffered only when I was acting dumb, sitting around so young I was sucking my thumb.

But now I've found that deep within, my soul has no doubt, and fear was just a tool that told me I was a fool. Alert and awake, I'm alive, real, and quite frankly a big deal. For I am a twinkle in my Lord's eye. When I feel and know this, I just can't blow this, for my life is a gift I freely give and receive and delight in. He has made me full of grace as a part of this human race.

The past storms of my life allowed me to grow deeper roots for this leg of my earthly journey here below. My home is Heaven above, but while I'm here, I'll have no fear, for His love is always near.

Amen!

_____
_____
_____
_____
_____

January 23

My soul is perfect, whole, and complete. That's quite a feat to realize I am that neat and free. My mind cannot hijack me because I'm surrounded by my Lord's glee, which will never flee. No illusion can create the confusion as I'm anchored with this truth deep within.

I am perfect, whole, and complete, and the souls that are earthly bound and surround me are internally filled with this light of love from God within and above.

I can feel You, which causes me to kneel and truly heal. Your love in me knows no bounds as I see through the veil, for Your love sustains, inspires, heals, connects, and delights me through all my flights in this gift of life.

Amen.

January 24

The love of God is in me. The only hope I need is this absolute truth. The source of love, life, wholeness, and joy is the source of this divine light. The eternal light of my soul. There are no earthly worries in the infinite. The source of creation and the created is this same light within.

May I let it shine in pure love, without judgment, with kindness and forgiveness extended even before a wrong is committed against me. May I receive this same forgiveness when I fall down and disappoint someone I was given to love. May I spend all my days in the full knowledge of You, Lord, and in the freedom of the light of love. You, oh Lord, my God, are my creator, sustainer, savior, and friend.

Amen!

January 25

A friend challenged me to comprehend the meaning and feeling of God's very love. He compared it to fish surrounded by water. We are immersed and surrounded in Love from the conductor of the train, the creator of the universe, the very inventor of love, the designer of Your soul.

Comprehend this true elation, share the height of this delight, take in the glory, be the light in Your own soul, and it will be obvious on Your face and will create the aura to all that You are the created of the creator of Love. Be the light of love magnified today and always as You, too, are reminded of whose You are. Try to comprehend the very nature, height, and depth of God's love as it's within me and You.

Amen!

January 26

Nobody knows me like You do, Lord, and yet You love me just the same. All the lessons, struggles, and joys are to call me home to You. In every heartache and tear, You had a wiser purpose for me to see my total need for You, a savior for a sinner that You declare a saint—that's me! May I enjoy and not endure the journey home to You.

I leave my heart open. I will follow Your spirit's leading. I can discern You directly from Your heart. You are gracious and the very definition of love. If I walk in the steps of love, I already have all I need. You are inside and at the center of my soul; You are the architect of my spirit. May I now move to the vibrations of Your true heart that become mine.

May I grow this day and every day on earth until I am just like You.

Amen!

January 27

Lord, You made me! I am of You! Prevent my doubting that I am not perfect like You as all of mankind is a miracle of Your mind.

Every wound, hurt, and doubt is merely a pathway that You are leading me home.

Every person I've loved who's gone beyond rests with You, adding to the loving calls when it's time for me to go.

I see You, Lord, at the finish line with the checkered flag specifically for me. But for now, You have souls for me to dance with and people to love, encourage, and even just to help pull through the day, walking next to them on their journey of life, faith, and love.

Lord, allow me to thrive as Your light in the darkness of my fellow journeyman on this walk to You, my God!

Show me how to love like You love me, Lord!

Amen!

January 28

Lord, I awake today with a clean heart from a deepened knowledge of the truth of Your Love. My spiritual heart is awakened with Love for myself because it's engineered by a new understanding of Your true love.

There is nothing and no one I cannot forgive, but it's me I have waited to forgive last. This reality is from You, Lord, who loves unconditionally beyond understanding. I can only experience Your love when I rest in You. This makes me whole because I am worthy as Your child. I cannot add to it but only live to realize fully who You are in me.

In this world, I work for perfection and holiness, thinking I need to earn my place, but it only cheapens what You already gave me: the gift of life.

I receive Your love and allow it to emanate through me to all You have given me to know, be surrounded by, and love!

Thank You, my Lord, for giving me Your very own love now without doubt so I can *be* Your love!

Amen!

January 29

Love cannot be used as a weapon because it's God's gift.

God gives me discernment to walk in the way of His love.

May I never judge in place of love as love is God's free gift that I receive.

Standing up to hate is not always convenient, but it's You in me that speaks. So, with the transforming power within me, I have the strength to speak out, not to condemn but invite others to Your love. For it's Your voice within that yells out for peace, harmony, and love that must be heard.

My perfect protection from evil is God's judgment. I am to love through it all, pointing to my source of love, God of all. Peace is the floral bouquet, and love is the bloom.

Love is sacred, as it is You and not an emotion or seduction but sacred words that reveal You in me.

May this be the practice of my life, Lord, in reflection of You.

Amen!

January 30

Lord, may I value purpose more than pleasure.

Prevent the fleeting distortions of the mind that attempt to replace this purpose of love. May I relish learning to be still in Your presence. Prevent my mind from being hijacked to less than what and who I am as Yours. When love is the magnet of my heart, there is nothing but love and nothing but God, who is perfect love.

When we focus on love, low vibrations can no longer exist in our realm.

My connection and energetic presence is light from the Lord. My Love for You, God, creates Ecstasy within me and Your delight without pretense.

May my only focus be to Love You with my whole mind, heart, body, and soul as the first, last, and ongoing agenda of each new day. Godly perpetual love!

Amen!

January 31

I am Your beloved; may I build myself up in Your holy faith. I pray that the Holy Spirit will keep me in the love of God, waiting for the mercy of our Lord eternally.

Dissolve my doubt, as fear cannot coexist in the presence of Your love. The intensity of Your love is always available to me when I rest and know that You are in control. My courage is the result of my increasing trust in You and letting go of my illusion of control.

So I release this tight grip that life's circumstances create as I learn that all I do and know is to grow in every way to be in Your perpetual light.

Amen!

FEBRUARY: PRAISE

February: Praise

February 1

Good morning, God! It's another day for me to grow and learn as I earn my way in this world. But what's most secure is my love from You, which You endlessly do and is without doubt true. So, when I get stuck in earthly ruts, I remember that You are the one who has prepared the way for me to be permanently with You.

Whether today is cheers or tears, I know there is no reason for fear because I take it all to You. I am through being blue when I focus the eyes of my heart on You.

So I look for this day to simply say: I am one with You!

Amen.

February 2

Lord, strengthen my faith. As fear and faith both cannot be seen, they require me to choose to believe. Since only one can prevail, I choose to rely upon faith in each and every hour. My false fear then fades as the security of Your holy embrace covers me like a warm blanket. It transforms me from fear to faith, with love blooming in full grace in this place. Love is Your light dissolving the darkness of fear. I cannot see it or often describe it, but it's that confidence of comfort that is the core of my soul, allowing me to be bold and never fold.

Faith shines within and guides me through until life's end.

Amen.

February 3

Thy will be done! When I pursue my own will, I find only chaos that I could have avoided. Yet You still free me and guide me, calling me to travel on the path of freedom. I discern Your beautiful expression of serenity that waits for me.

You never give up on me; Your call is always before me. As each new day brings new trials, I realize that Your perfection frees me from worry and doubt.

Nothing is up to me, as You have created my life how it's meant to be. May peace and trust expand through my thoughts surrendered to You.

Amen.

February 4

My way to change the world is to change my mind about the world. I look to You, who guides me to Your beauty at work all around me. You open the eyes of my heart to see and reflect Your light even through the darkest of nights.

For there is no darkness where my soul shines, creating eternal, perfect sight.

Amen.

February 5

May my life be a path wiring my Heaven-bound mind. For here, peace will increase. In times of my own despair, Your grace opened the door for wisdom to say hello. These trials that I saw as my enemy are actually my soul's teacher.

Everything is created with the light of God that wastes nothing, as any negative thoughts I have become lessons.

For You have told me that the kingdom of God is in me. So when I doubt and allow shame to show itself, Your light of truth gives it the boot.

When I accept Your truth, I'm not far from the ecstasy Heaven will bring.

Amen!

February 6

I praise Your name, for You have done wonderful things!

I'm shaking off my old attitude with renewed gratitude to meet this day with Heavenly hope—for Your name is holy, and You have done great things for me.

I often don't see how great You are, but when I do, I can cure any mental flu. When my heart is open, my mind only knows the truth of You in me.

Your light of love dissolves fake fear that was only in my mind. With this reality, I charge ahead in first gear as I steer towards Your love!

Amen!

February 7

May I unburden my being of the thought that I'm performing for You. You are my best friend, freely accepting all I am as I am.

When doubt comes back, disharmony fills my soul until I remember that Your love is whole and complete, beyond all feats.

For when I simply open my heart, I am rid of doubt, free to shout, "My God, My God, it's ME with Your light of love in my heart as I know, accept, and receive. It's You inside me!"

Amen!

February 8

May I always be of good cheer as You have commanded, truly desiring it in my actions and not just parroting what I've been told to do.

If I don't block the negative thoughts, this cheer unnecessarily becomes fear.

But when I feel God's love, the energy who created rainbows, mountains, oceans, and trees, I realize He saved His best work to create me! I can lift up reverent praises to Him. In this, I feel the beam from His light to reflect His full delight.

Amen.

February 9

You are the light of the world! You are the spark when it's dark. You are my hope when doubt floods my mind. I find Your promise of eternal light that will remain in me to the end of the world. Help me remember to be the child You sent me to be, shining for all Your creation.

You are the light of the world!

Amen.

February 10

Lord, when I rest in my breath in You, every moment is made anew. With Your vision and the realization of Your lasting preservation, I am confident in Your provision. This reality frees me to focus on collaboration as a celebration of life, elevating me to elation. I feel your glow when I am guided by Your spirit.

As the flow of loving kindness is all I know and want to show, it's beautifully contagious to share with all I've come to care and know. All this renewed energy makes me certain of my acceptance in Your presence.

All I do now is with this confidence in mind, girding me from an earthly grind. For my ever-present find is that God is always on my mind. You are with me, within me, and Your presence is my deepest healing and always will be.

Amen!

February 11

My faith in You is my strength!
   There is no burden You will not lift.
   Your love is complete and waits patiently for me.
   You are my love and grace, with me at all times and in all places and spaces.
   When I trust as I must, You reign in me perfectly.
   No one can then cause me to doubt or question Your amazing, unshakable, and complete love.
   It's Your gift of peace and love that anchors me.
   I draw to You and forgive those who have ever caused me to doubt what you're all about. Your love for all Your people, whom You shower with grace and love, washes away any uncertainty. May doubt be as far as the east is from the west as I shout from the rooftops with glee that anything lesser should flee.
   You, my God, wash away fear and disbelief with Your mercy, grace, and love.
   My energy of strength comes from You in me.

Amen!

_____
_____
_____
_____
_____
_____
_____
_____

February 12

You are a happy God!

Remind me not to be crappy. I see You! You conceived for me to take joy in You, allowing my spirit to be a happy boy filled with joy. It's not just a ploy for my mind to really know Your joy. I am free to be one with You as I meditate on the good You do.

I breathe in the miracle of life that is my freedom to be Your very own joy. You give it, I receive it, so I truly believe it. In this moment, I choose not to snooze as that's the only way to lose. I will now be inhaling life that begins in my heart from the start. This frees me of any past that haunts, taunts, and no longer flaunts. Count on me to choose to be free. After all, IT'S UP TO ME! This Godly joy lives in me if I call it to be free. Often, I forget to just let it flow where Your happiness grows.

My energy is dependent on my heart's engine. I attach a Heavenly jumper cable to keep me stable. I have new energy when my mind is free to be alive and strives to be Yours. It's simple to feel alive when I jump-start this heart.

God, please remind me to reprogram my mind to be aware of You. In each moment, reawaken me to be free and see that glee. After all, it's You who surrounds me.

Amen.

_____
_____
_____
_____

February 13

You generously poured out Your spirit on me. I have become new through this grace. It cleanses me, shields me, and calls me.

It gives me strength when I am weak. It protects me at the peak of day and guides me in my need for rest, especially when I have fallen. Then, all I have to do is confess and recognize Your love for me is true. Then I am Restored, Revived, Revitalized. You endlessly welcome me back to the fold just as You foretold.

Amen!

February 14

Lord, once I learned my life is a gift from You and not a contest with man, I was awakened. I began to see mysteries and miracles with new glee.

God, You are good to me as Your patience is beyond the concept of my mind. You've lifted me from man's grime to the sublime. I'm done with doubt and disbelief, renewed by thee at this time.

When my mind is quiet and no longer controls my energy, my spirit is alive and in automatic drive for me to truly thrive. This minimizes projection and jealousy, replacing it with delight in the unique plan You designed for me.

God, You are for me, for You are always good to me even when I don't see. You are always expanding my soul, the eternal me. Your love melts fear, bringing permanent peace and creating a new reality.

Amen!

_____
_____
_____
_____
_____
_____
_____
_____
_____
_____

February 15

Lord, I woke up, and now I get it! When I stop struggling as a man, I start living as a spirit. When I commune as a spirit, the ego's war depletes and no longer denies me perfect peace, love, and harmony. Your plan is to lead me to abundance through Your grace. No ego could conjure wealth, status, or position apart from You; that is all scarcity in disguise.

But scarcity turns to abundance when it's received as Your gift of provision. This joy is merely accepting the unique gift You created just for ME. Just as You do perfectly and uniquely by Your mighty touch for all!

Let us rejoice and not compare and JUST be GLAD in Your gifts for me and my brother and sister!

Amen!

February 16

May the river of Your spirit run through me so the overflow of my life is You. May I become a lantern of Your comfort by just being.
Might this light be a path for those I know.
Let Your presence be felt in the energy that unites all the faithful.
Lord, it is the day to bring Your peace to the hearts that I've been given to share.
Praise our Lord God!

Amen!

February 17

My blessing is on the horizon. My faith assures me this truth is an absolute promise from my Father in Heaven!

There is no tear that does not transform to blessing, and life's realized blessings are each magnified. Every tear turns into a diamond of the heart, and my grief turns into the tight grip of God around my arms.

My sadness is the foundation for Heaven's launchpad to elation.

Every kindness I extended to every homeless person—each smile and blessing—surrounds me for the most epic party in the Heavens.

Our souls jointly dance with delight, and our songs are in perfect harmony. God Himself and a legion of His angels dance, sing, and delight fully in each other as we are in the full presence of God's love.

All earthly grievances are vanquished and pave the way for freedom in full forgiveness, full pardon, as we are God's children come HOME!

There will be a fatted calf, golden ring, and purple royal robe for EACH of US. You and me!

Hallelujah!

_____
_____
_____
_____
_____
_____

February 18

God's love for me is revealed with total clarity in the life, birth, death, and resurrection of Jesus. God Himself became fully man so that we could relate to, see, feel, and be just like Him, perfect in grace and forgiveness. I will grant myself freedom and joy, leading to unconditional love, because the origin of this amazing gift I have is from the fullness of the trinity. God coming as man, Jesus covering the cost of my sin, and the holy spirit within to allow His very own love to live in me forevermore.

He did this for me. I know now the real truth of unconditional love.

I can love others; I can overcome judgment and comparison, leaving only equality. The love I know comes from the ultimate source and creator of love who dwells within me!

Amen!

February: Praise

February 19

Lord God, You are my rock and my fortress. You never forsake me. When I am confused, You are not. When I am struggling, Your hand holds me upright. When I am weak, You are my strength.

I am often blind to Your constant steadfast love, but You restore my sight. You are my clarity in confusion. You fill me with Your love when I can't seem to bring my heart to love when I'm in despair. When I lose my way and become angry, You reach to the depth of my soul and shine Your light of renewal to transition me back to love. When I wait upon You, all things are new, fresh, and restored.

When I'm in sorrow, Your very own spirit cracks that sorrow to reveal Your eternal hope. When I am lost, You give me directions and surround me with Your other children who know the way. You never leave me, even when I feel alone. You are always there above me, below me, and within me.

Thank You, my gracious, all-loving, and forgiving God of mercy who never tires, never gives up on me, and makes all things new. I see You, I feel You, I rest in You and Your promises to me.

May my heart rest in this absolute truth, and may I share these healing truths with all mankind who You have created, loved, and are calling all the time just like me. Thank You!

Amen!

_____
_____
_____
_____

February 20

Lord God, You are my source of love within my spirit.

Mold my heart! May the fingerprints of Your hand remain upon it as fresh as when You placed it within my being.

May this allow revenge to give way to forgiveness, pride to humility, and separation to harmony that allows a new depth of unity in my community.

May I desire to serve others, not needing approval from anyone but You within me.

My delight will be in the confidence of who I am in You.

My joy comes from my freedom, as a bird who discovered that the birdcage never had a door but was always open.

May I be still in Your presence and radiate the knowledge of freedom in You, Lord!

Amen!

February 21

Reign in me, Lord. May I glorify You where I go.

Fill me with Your kindness overflowing.

The joy inside of me is irrefutable, a testament to experiencing Your joy and delight.

I do not look for You because where I am there, You are, too. I am reminded of Your glory and magnificence when I simply see and experience Your presence in those I come to know. When I go to meet in public places, there I find You. When I rest at home, it's Your presence that I find nourishment and rest in.

All I hope to know, do, and experience is joy when I know it's You being revealed in all I do and everywhere I go.

Praise You, my Lord, master, Father, and friend!

Amen!

February 22

Make a joyful noise and be glad. Lord, may You call me to great harmony in the day. May You bring healing of trauma to this land and be gracious, Lord.

Might Your mercy be plentiful, and may Your very own joy reign in me today.

May my ears be open and my heart turned toward others and remain soft.

May I, through You, be a joy giver, creating unity through harmony!

Amen!

February 23

God in Heaven, creator of all, You know me by name and created every detail within. Each celebration and struggle were both created and allowed by Your touch of creation for my good and Your glory.

Allow me to see that everything that happens around me and in me is for the greater good as I walk on this pathway of life. May I understand fully that all of life and my death to come are equal parts of my eternity. That I am not waiting to be with You as You are with me and in me, now and always were.

You are the delight and the light that I know and see. It is You who walks me from the edge of the cliff of life for my growth and goodness.

How can I feel less than or not enough when I am Your crowning creation?

Allow me to feel, know, and share this true delight. When I am weary, remind me; when I'm weak, strengthen me; when I'm lost, allow me to feel found in Your presence.

Lord of all, reign in me in such a way that passing emotions only restore me to the full knowledge of Your presence within.

Oh, I give thanks to You, Lord, for Your steadfast love endures FOREVER!

Amen!

_____
_____
_____
_____

February 24

The dew of Heaven brings Your joy to earth every morning.

My Lord, You refresh my spirit with the first morning breath of air, filling my lungs with the freshness of Your love.

Your sunlight brings Your golden rays upon my shoulders, reawakening me every day.

Lord, I am in You. My vibrance within my mind is the meaning You instill within me, even before the days my feet walked the earth.

You have every breath counted that I will breathe before I return to Your perfect, peaceful presence.

My joy is indescribable, my peace is powerful, and my rest is in the delight of Your being.

Thank You, my God and friend, for I fully delight in You.

Amen.

February 25

From the rising of the sun to its setting, the name of the LORD is to be praised!

Your truth in Your words guides me as a new creation.

As I praise Your name, You rest in my spirit. I fully receive Your blessings.

God of all comfort, You are fully pleased in my trust in You.

I feel free, new, and whole every morning. At night, I rest with knowledge of Your full delight in me.

Joyful tears in my eyes gently wash away darkness and illusions in my mind that created false separation in me from Your perfection, beauty, and love.

I am in You, Lord, resurrected in spirit and prepared to be Your joy giver.

Amen!

February 26

The Lord freed me! No longer am I a slave to ambition, attention, or pleasure.

All of these are empty, deceitful lies to deter my beauty, perfection, and natural design. I allowed the poison of my mind to infect my spirit, but now the lessons of living cleanse me.

Instead, I delight in the reality of the light of truth.

I am not man-made, but as God made, I'm creation's design. Eternally living, not waiting, but just now BEING.

I am a rock! A boulder does not compare its might, worth, weight, or value to a stone. It rests perfectly in togetherness and stillness, just being a foundation of God's creation, for its purpose is to stand in strength forevermore. I am, so I will!

Amen!

_____
_____
_____
_____
_____
_____
_____
_____
_____
_____
_____
_____
_____

February 27

I am so blessed. I am so grateful. I am love. I need no explanation, just an expression from my soul.

After all, I am to be Your blessing to the world. Your love surrounds me to remind me so I'm whole and healthy. In You, all things are well in all circumstances!

Pain and peace live on the same street.

I just need to decide which driveway to park in. You have chosen to show me which was reserved in my name.

There is nothing for me to say, then thank You, God. Thank You!

Amen!

February 28

May my faith be great! Give me a strengthening of faith in my trust of You so my doubt erodes and my trust expands.

May Your healing energy flow through me, bringing peace that replaces my confusion.

May the laws not cause me to be a slave of self-judgment. After all, it is my faith that frees me. May my struggle to comprehend this melt to a simple understanding that allows me to love You in a way that grace abounds from You through me.

Just as Your radiant sun shines upon my face, may the moon glow in the darkness to guide my way. There is both the sun and the moon guiding me day and night, constantly reminding me I never walk alone or in total darkness, and I am always in Your guidance.

You have set me in a constant light to illuminate Your love. Even when it's in the dim of the night, it shines so bright in proportion to my love for You, God!

It is for freedom that You have freed me. Set me free from the thoughts that keep my sight limited in seeing the fullness of Your glory. Give me strength in my weakness; be my compass when I feel lost.

Keep me far from the burdens of my mind. Your Love is the light that illuminates my soul within as You hold me in Your perfect love.

Amen!

_____
_____
_____
_____

MARCH: BROTHERLY LOVE

March: Brotherly Love

March 1

Lord, You said, "Do not be afraid," because fear blocks Love, and You are the Author of Love.

May I reflect Your book of love endlessly in what I say and do. May I see everyone that I meet with the Heavenly perception that circles around me. When my mind takes off in flight, I lose my anchoring in You, and fear creeps in, blocking Your light and creating a dark night. But I look to You, and suddenly, Your love creates an everlasting light—my hope through the night.

So, Lord, give me the ability to recognize fear when it deceitfully knocks at my door. It does not block reality but awakens my spirit to Your presence. I start anew, knowing Love was always there.

Take fear from me, and let love be ever-present, overflowing, and always growing!

Amen!

_____
_____
_____
_____
_____
_____
_____
_____
_____
_____

March 2

Abiding in Your love is the only way I can truly love, not by imitating You but by surrendering. I can only give what I take in of You. So help me, Lord, to receive Your love abiding in me. May I love from You within. Free me from the blockages of judgment and of self-condemnation so I can live and love unconditionally. You have been so kind and good to me. May I be the same to others. I couldn't earn it or deserve it, but You gave Yourself to me in Your absolute love. May I believe it, be it, receive it, and practice it!

Amen.

March: Brotherly Love

March 3

Lord God, allow me this day to connect spiritually with Reid on his birthday. While these writings I share I hear as whispers from him . . . today, it's I who hope to be heard by Reid.

The heartache from your Heavenly departure is one that can never heal, but the love we have for you no one can ever steal.

Your courage and honesty can still be felt with the grace of love you lived by. I distinctly remember your dance upon the earth, the proof of your desire to believe, see, inspire, inquire, and encourage.

I know of no other who could speak as corrective and loving intertwined as you could—and still do.

You inspire me every day to become more forgiving and loving than you knew me. But your life has inspired me to take a higher road than I have ever known. So, on this, your birthday, I say thank you to the present moment to awaken my soul to the highest level of positivity I could ever know. For through you, I can see Heaven's light on my earthly path.

Happy Birthday, Reid!

_____
_____
_____
_____
_____
_____
_____

March 4

The reality of You, Lord within, is Your ability to use us to heal one another. May I be the calm that cures the stirs of the world's heartache. But when I meet it with Your constant peace, which is always available to me, it lifts me and others to new heights.

This feeling is found for no obvious reason as it's not a special season. But my mind sends the signal to be calm, confident, and present. It's then I know my connection is Your projection. I receive it, believe it, and heal with it.

Amen.

March 5

I have no right to withhold God's love. I have a responsibility to receive it, bathe in it, and allow it to spill over wherever I go. Forgive me for ever thinking I don't deserve it, as that is what was wrongly taught to me. I am God's child, made for the purpose to love. Be love. Live love. To love from my soul and recognize, experience, see, share, and be this very love to and through me.

The freedom is in knowing and showing freely His love that is in me and seeing that identical love in all who surround me.

Amen!

March 6

EVERYONE is a friend of the beloved.
That's the magic and mystery of my heart.
But harmony is disrupted when I forget I am walking between two worlds. In this age of revenge, resentment, grievance, and jealousy, we are sheep following inherited hatred. I stand staring at two possibilities of realities: my love of Christ and my love of the world.
My soul thirsts for the reminder that God gave us an uncorrupted soul so we can lift people out of the pit by reawakening the God within.
We cannot forget that love is reflected within us.
So I will not dwell on the malaise but will rise with the Holy Spirit within.
Today, I oppose the incoming attacks; I will resist nothing but will captivate all with Your beauty. My heart shall not fear, for You are near, and Your mighty army is constantly at my side.

Amen.

_____
_____
_____
_____
_____
_____
_____
_____
_____

March 7

You have written Your truth, hope, and love on my heart. Everything may look like it's in disarray, but with You, I can journey through and know You are always true. You have been reflected on my heart from the start!

My privilege is my perseverance in representing You. For where love is found, I'm duty-bound to recognize that it's You. This recognition gives me my mission to represent You and love the others all around me.

Amen.

March 8

I'm only truly loving another when I accept them just as they are. It's not up to me to change anyone or see through my ego's eyes but simply to see them from my Lord's lens.

My growth is in deeply trusting that the God who made me has a perfect plan for me and for all mankind.

So the greatest lesson for the depth of my being is to overcome worldly division. May I know the unity dissolving earthly judgment, control, or pity, and see nothing but Godly potential in me and all those around. May the evolution of my spirit allow me to fully delight in the success of others, freeing me from egoic jealousy. Instead, I want others to uplift the universe with their gifts and generosity.

I receive serenity and no longer believe in hierarchy, for that is malarkey keeping me from being whole. Everyone is a gift who can lift others up!

May I love with freeing love that heals, enlightens, and forgives.

Amen.

March 9

You, Lord, love me so. May I truly understand this depth.

I desire to trust that You are there before me on my earthly road. May I come to know that the delight in life is to be a blessing to others as that energy creates serenity.

My wounds are healed as I'm used to heal others.

This boomerang of the Love You authored calls me to experience it unselfishly. I stand in this line of humanity, created to share and bear every care of my community as You design this unity.

The beauty that's possible in me, I now see is You in Me!

Amen.

March 10

Lord of mercy, my love is Your energy in me, waiting to be released. When I bestow my love here below, I become more like thee!

I'm free to be all You meant for me.

To be an expression of Your love, I need to humbly receive Your love, eliminating my pride so negativity can't hide. You gave me this earthly life to learn and discern Your beautiful truths that now fortify me.

So, as I grow old, I won't need to be told God's love is bold because it's fully realized inside me!

Amen!

_____
_____
_____
_____
_____
_____
_____
_____
_____
_____
_____
_____
_____
_____

March 11

May I increase my joy by sharing it with others.
You are the guard of my peace at the door of my mind and at the foundation of my heart.
Though Your call increases in my moments of struggle, it is also constant. I pray that I might increasingly be a reflection of Your love through the kindness You lead me to share. As I release the ego in me, call me to Your intended beauty and Your eternal unity.
In You, I have Your spirit of protection to wash away fear. I have Your strength to tame all my weaknesses. You are my comfort and healer; Your spirit is my constant companion. I desire to live in unity with all Your children.
My strength is in the power of Your might, for You are this sheep's Shepard. When my spirit is down or weakness lurks, Your restoration flows through me in harmony.
I am strong in Your restorative power, enabling me to lift my own spirit as I share Your unfailing love with others.

Amen.

March 12

May I be cheerful, for that is the flowering of health. Call me this morning to kindness as that is the wealth of the mind.

May gratitude flow freely from me. I hope to empathize with my fellow men so I can encourage them with my words.

Might I use them to encourage and understand how others in this land receive and believe by the love I give.

As I greet new faces and hear their voices, might my energy be comforting to them so they become a good friend.

Amen.

March 13

Love always wins. I have Your love in me and in all I see.

At my core, I receive Your light. May I see it knowing it will ultimately be the only thing surrounding me. Might I lose judgment that prevented me from seeing this potential for love in those who frightened me. Maybe it was my jealousy. The antidote to this fault in me is to recognize the flicker of light that You created in each soul around me.

I am now awake to the truth that Your love is everywhere I look. And through the struggles in my time, I learned I am worth more than a dime because I am a child of the divine. All I need to do is be aware of the love that waits around me, granted by my Father in Heaven.

Amen!

March 14

You are the Father of mercies and the God of all comfort. Your comfort is what equips me to comfort those that surround me. They need the same nourishment as me to carry on.

In each new day, Your presence renews me with the fresh morning air and with the song of hope in the birds' flight that demonstrates their morning might. You have made me Your coauthor of this morning's story. May I feel Your compassion and pass it on.

I am present with thee with an open heart, ready to be a golden glow that flows to each soul that walks alongside mine. You are in me to celebrate the gift of life, and with each beat of the heart, I feel You flowing in me.

Thank You for each miracle and for the blessings of those who enrich my life.

Use me to be a joy of life that eliminates strife. I appreciate everything, both the gifts that encourage and the challenges that stretch me to be all You planned for me.

Gratitude fills my heart as beauty from You surrounds me so.

Amen!

March 15

May I offer the medicine of mercy to those I meet. I should not be prone to judge or shame but free to express God's love that surpasses all understanding.

Give me the ability to respond with love and with the peace from a dove to the earthly attacks and trauma within. I pray that love transcends from You to me to all of the human attacks upon me. May mercy and compassion be my instinct rather than judgment and revenge. For in Your order, grace is never met with disgrace as giving is receiving.

Beyond the ego's wounds and deceit of my mind that is perfectly transformed in the beauty of the divine.

It is peace, harmony, and unity that You most desire for my neighbor and me. So be it! So it is, and it will be!

This mercy is for all of Your children, just like me.

Amen!

_____
_____
_____
_____
_____
_____
_____
_____
_____
_____
_____
_____

March 16

God loves us, so it should be easy for me to love all others.

Instead of the differences, I should immediately see unity. In my heart, I know God's best for me, but sometimes, there's interference in the transmission from my heart to my head. With a soft, receiving heart, may I overcome my need to prove I'm smart. That short-traveling emotion and thought often find the enemy of ego in between the two, giving me a mental flu.

But all I have to do is know You're preparing my heart to be perfectly one with thee. When I fall short, it's only a minor tort as You are my support on life's ball court.

You have my days counted until I'm perfected in the full grace and light of Your mercy, which cleans me from all blight. In time, I'll be free of all crime, perfect in Your midst eternally.

Amen!

March: Brotherly Love

March 17

God of mercy, Lord of grace, I am in this place, waiting for my Heavenly space.

My trials are in the here and now and often with the people I should easily be able to commend and be a friend without pretending.

Give me a renewed ability to calmly build unity.

The differences among us are minimized when my reactions are not super-sized.

I find myself at a loss when the arrows of division are headed at me. So might my ego not be the first to respond and instead bend to get along.

Lord, before I speak, when confrontation abounds and threatens a frown, might I calm down. Convict my spirit and tame my tongue with an ability to say nothing at all. I want to speak only what's true, beneficial, and kind, not just a roar in my own mind.

May I act in accordance with Your example. I'm kind and polite, not looking for a fight.

May I give and receive with this ability to please.

Amen!

_____
_____
_____
_____
_____
_____

March 18

Ideas create possibilities. Lord, allow me to see the magic of this day. May the strength of the Lord empower me today for all that is good. May I be holy as You created me. May I see and help the hurting. May I be near to the joy-filled to magnify their light. I am Your peace poured out to Your people. I am lovable because I am Your expression of life.

I choose love fueled by who I am in You, for this is why I am created by You, the creator. May I simply be a reflection of You today!

Amen.

March 19

Lord, I delight in You! I deepen my heart of compassion so that I might love more like You. Lord, I shed fear for faith so I can be strong like You. Lord, I freely give pieces of my heart to others to have understanding like You. Lord, I delight in You so I can have joy like You. Lord my God, I'm just like You! I'm able to fully delight when my eyes are upon You, for all I need and all I am or meant to be was to be just like You! This is not something I have to wait for but can embrace right now, from the moment You created me by Your thought and breath. I'm a reflection of You, for I was made by You and for You.

Now I know I can fully delight in You in Your constant presence. Keep open the hearts of our souls, for I want to be just like You.

Amen!

March 20

Lord, allow me to be blessed by being a blessing to others. May my strength be renewed by the smiles I create, the hope I instill, and the life I give. May I receive the energy of Heaven as I encourage Your children, and might my joy increase as I practice selflessness and kindness today.

Take away the things that create distance from others. Might my ego melt to meet, submit, and magnify the spirit within. Help me to forgive the ways I've been wronged and create kindness over forgiveness. May the Love in me be the winner today and dissolve the heavy feelings that cause distance between me and others.

The only thing that matters is that I carry Your love and share it. May the mistakes of yesterday be erased and prevent a heaviness today. Today is completely new, so fill it with fresh starts, creating new possibilities of humility and unity, replacing distance and arrogance. May I be Your light of life through encouragement today.

Amen!

March 21

Lord God, crack my ego of shame and the lies that make me miss the miracle of You that I AM! Make my soul free. I am no longer a prisoner to lies but a delight to my very own soul and to You, my GOD, companion, and friend.

May this condition within my spirit be contagious. I want to be inspired so that I can inspire. Use the energy and euphoria from You that is now deep within me, Lord. Prevent the world from extinguishing it, and may I remain sensitive and be a light, ensuring I don't dim the flame in others.

May I feel God's love and be able to convey feelings in my description, allowing Your presence to be felt in my encounters. May my image to others be Your spirit within me, for we are one in spirit and in truth. When I own and know this, I am free! I am You to others.

As I encourage, might I also be encouraged. That's not selfish; that's Your design to magnify our joy in You!

So be it!

Amen!

March 22

God's goodness surrounds me and fills me. May Your light of encouragement be contagious through me as a reflection of Your spirit in me, Lord. May I be a testament of love to all others I come to know, without words but by my actions of charity and kindness.

Lord, give me the will and ability to hear others more than I wish to be heard. May You be evident in me by my compassion to Your children, who You have blessed me to influence. May I fully delight in Your will, and may my service be pleasing to You and a blessing to those You bless through me.

I humbly commit this prayer to Your service.

Amen!

March 23

Lord of Heaven and Earth, the God of all creation, create this day's journey to be one of purpose and passion. May it be submersed in Your presence. May the words I speak uplift and the steps I take bring me nearer to You. May the things I hear magnify You in my life. Remind me to remain teachable with all others who speak from Your voice. I want to fully delight in who I am in You today.

Surround me with people who direct my path toward You. May I reflect Your presence by instinctively following You. Use me to encourage and awaken myself and others to Your magnificence. Might I radiate the warmth of Your presence to those I'm with today. Your very own energy will be my radiance.

Open the eyes of my heart to see the good I can do and the encouragement I can bring to the hurting. Inspire me to awaken those asleep to Your love. Thank You, for You have promised that if I ask, I shall receive. So shall it be. May I, who am imperfect, be used by You, a perfect God.

Amen!

_____
_____
_____
_____
_____
_____
_____

March 24

Lord, my desire is to do as You have instructed: love You, the Lord my God, with all my mind, heart, and soul.
    And Love others as myself.
    The first is the easiest, for You are perfect, glorious, and all good comes from You. But the second causes me to struggle as others frustrate, confuse, compare, and judge. May I overcome these difficulties, freeing me of judgment, comparison, and division. No hate has ever conquered hate; only love extinguishes hate. May I feel the freeing nature of Your spirit descend on me and fall into my soul.
    Free me from the struggle to love myself and free me of self-judgment, the condemning voice in my head. Then, I can love myself and accept the truths and authenticity You have gifted me with. When I make this transformation, my internal love is freely extended to others. For if I cannot truly love myself, I have no source to extend this love. What sounds selfish is the only freedom from which I can love others.
    Lord, I now understand loving myself is loving You within, and loving others is seeing and loving You, who is also within them. If I live by the spirit, this is automatic; if I live by ego, this is impossible as it separates and isolates. I'm free to love others when I see the soul You created and breathed into my existence was, is, and will be just as You designed.
    When the self-critical inner eye ceases, my outward eye sees my brother and sister with love and not judgment and the freedom to give what I know in You: love, forgiveness, and grace. I see now through Your eyes as You guide the eyes of my heart to look at others with grace, mercy, and joy, as it all comes from You through me for others.

March: Brotherly Love

In You, with real love for myself, I can now live with real love easily pouring out of me for others. Harmony, unity, and true inner peace!

Amen!

March 25

Awaken me! Awake me, my Lord. When I feel the pain of others, and I comfort them, I heal as their wounds mend. When I am surrounded with those who are asleep, may I remain awake and be their watchman. May I be blessed to be a blessing to the grief-stricken, the homeless, the fatherless, the addicted, the lonely, and the lost.

May I be worthy of being taken advantage of and used, and may I not need to be thanked. For this is what it means to be Your hands and feet: to remember all the wounds You healed in me and how You provided abundance even when I lived in scarcity.

Make me Your very own love, God, for those I know and come to know. When I am in a state of compassion, empathy, and forgiveness, I experience a glimpse of Your kindness, forgiveness, love, and grace.

If my heart is focused on love and my heart given to be Your care, I can't help but see You in those around me.

May each of us be reminded of You and Your love as we dance with the souls on earth that You have given us to be with!

So be it!

Amen!

_____
_____
_____
_____
_____
_____

March 26

I know the goodness of God. My true reality is peace through the truth of my Lord and creator. There is not one day of separation from the love of the Lord. There are days I close my eyes, choose not to recognize it, and feel the illusion of separation and isolation. When I forget, I just have to remember that all of life is teaching me that I'm not a body; I'm a spirit. I have the promise that my soul's resting place is eternally in the intense light of love with my Lord, God, and King.

My permanent place is a part of divinity in Heaven, as my place in humanity is only while on earth. I awaken to the promises of God. His harmony and permanent presence of peace were always there, waiting for the eyes of my heart to open. I just need to awaken my soul and receive from the joy giver.

His perfect love meets my every need. I must have the humility to receive with an open heart and the unspeakable joy to delight in sharing Heaven's euphoric energy. Then, I can love, encourage, and be God's love to others. Wow, I get to heal and encourage others to laugh and experience joy that only magnifies mine when I see, know, experience, and practice, mimicking my Lord's role as Joy Giver. The more I give, the more I experience God's love.

I am an immortal soul that cannot be harmed as my personality gives into the consciousness of my soul. I am a soul, not just an earthly body. A Heaven-made eternal soul formed by God's own complete light of love.

Delight fully into eternity and beyond. It's what God had in mind all along. The illusion of struggle gives way to the surpassing peace, which is me!

Amen!

Whispers From Heaven

March 27

God, allow me to imitate You. Use my mind to mend my soul and, thereby, give me words of love to nourish the walking wounded on earth. May I mark success with souls I've nourished rather than the wallets I've filled. Allow my spirit to dance with other souls simply to declare my delight in You.

Free me of self-judgment, and may I call out to You daily to accept and receive Your gift of freedom for my life in You. May I see others more nearly to my own soul with the ability to see You more clearly in both them and me.

Reawaken the child-like innocence in me and the ability to love unconditionally and innocently, just like my dog, Taffy. All who come are received with expectation of goodness. Fear of no one and pure love poured out and received. May I be naive enough to replace judgment with acceptance and condemnation with forgiveness. Allow me to know, as I was recently reminded by a friend, that setbacks are setups for God to bring me my greatest comeback.

In You I trust, now and always!

Amen!

March 28

Lord, make me a river of Your love. May Your spirit pour through me to others as Your energy of love is not a reservoir but is freely flowing. May the riverbank grid the boundaries that direct the overflow to the lives You have given me to be a blessing to.

May my life create harmony in the community of faith.

May the voice of my soul be pleasing to Your ears and be soothing to those who thirst for peace.

May the time You have given me encourage, bless, and create the sweetness of Your presence.

Amen!

March 29

Lord, free my eternal soul to be the true source of my love. As a soul is only capable of love. In this, there is no judgment in my being as it is my bridge to compassion, empathy, and unconditional love for myself and others.

The bonds of the heart are engineered by You, my God, as my soul is eternal, and those we love and who love us from their soul are always with us. There is no separation here or in Heaven. In judgment, I create separation, which only leads to misery and isolation, products of the physical, but when perfected in my soul, only harmony exists.

May I develop compassion and see the soul of others as no soul is less then. May I desire to be a bridge of healing to clashing cultures, which feed the ego of man and shield me and others from the love my soul has to give. May I learn to accept love and compassion, and may it grease the skids of my soul to naturally extend it.

God, You are love. I wish to be, in my spirit, just like You. After all, God within is who I am . . . God with us.

Amen!

March 30

You are and always were LOVE. You are Lord! Not a distant King on a throne upon high but Lord of my life, my heart, and this world.

I'm to be a reflection of this truth of Your love. Not to preach it or proclaim it but allow You to be seen in it, allowing You of Your love within to be heard through my silence and the smile of my soul to be revealed to those I come to know. This is the way for them to know You through me. I am truly alive only when magnifying Your love.

So often, I have been confused and felt I must learn and earn my way. But even before my birth, You decided to bring me upon this earth with the hope that I would learn to be Your love left behind through me to Your other children, who are also, for now, left behind. We are not alone; we are Yours and together in this place and time as You are here in me and the others as I come to see.

The material things can bless or condemn. It's a question of "Do they bless me, or do they own me? Are they mine, or am I theirs?"

Misery is found both in the hearts of the rich and poor.

Joy is found in God's boundless unconditional love, so it's in trust of You, Lord. Then, I can fully receive lasting joy and peace, whether I am rich or poor. Because I've found I am just simply Yours!

Amen!

_____
_____
_____
_____

March 31

Lord God, may I love because You are the breath in my lungs. May I stop "trying" to be worthy of Your love. You made me, created me, and breathed me into life with Your breath of Love.

Take from me judgment, comparison, and separation. Quiet my mouth and slow me in seeing and speaking the imperfections in others and self-criticism of myself. We are Your children, just growing up on this side of Heaven.

A dear friend of mine shared the sermon series in her church that spoke to me deeply. "I gave You one Job," to love one another! So simple yet so profound.

God's love will take off like an inferno and burn in each of us as we simply love one another and leave the rest to our God! He's got this in each of us. He is the author of my story from Him to each of us, and if I surrender to love, it is then through me.

I am a child of God; therefore, I was born to love from His very own heart.

God planted this one rule deep within my heart. May I practice it radically!

Amen in Your love!

_____
_____
_____
_____
_____
_____

APRIL: GOD'S BEAUTIFUL CREATION

April: God's Beautiful Creation

April 1

The rustle of the wind, the mist of the sea, the leaves on the tree all reveal Your majesty. My creator, savior, sustainer, and friend are always here within.

When I am challenged, You lift me. All I need to do is open the eyes of my heart to do my part and recognize Your majesty.

Miracles abound from the very ground. You breathed it all into existence with Godly persistence for which I have no resistance.

Your mysteries are all to be celebrated and discovered in Your creation. For You are constantly reminding me of who You are in me.

Amen.

April 2

I awake to see the sun's rays glisten on the surface of Your earth. It opens my heart to this new day as I greet this view that's my proof of You.

You have given so many reminders of Your majesty in all that surrounds me.

When the earthly frost makes my mind get lost, all I must do is look up and be renewed by YOU!

The moment my mind tries to start on its own, my heart reminds it that I am not separate from You. All my thoughts should exist to serve only You, not my imperfect desires. Now, from the eyes of my heart, I clearly see Your incredible majesty.

Amen!

April 3

Forgive me, for I was not awake or even truly alive; I was listening to lies. So much in motion and creating commotion, I missed the essence of Your presence: to be neighborly and welcome both the tall and the small. For everyone is worthy and should not be forlorn. So as long as it is up to me, I will live expectantly to welcome all in the spirit of love with peace like a dove.

I could not see the beauty in the whole darn tribe as I projected my insecurities and competed for favor. All I had to do was receive the belonging You offer, so now I see it's not too late for me. I'm still here.

Everyone has a specialty within to share and behold. Some are quiet, like a pearl inside the shell that's waiting to gel.

So my heart's wide open to bless the world, reversing the mess.

I can do my part to love from the start, straight from my heart.

So I smile to rid the vile, for it's more fun to beguile.

Amen!

April 4

Your peace guards my heart and mind. When my mind was slow to know this peace, it blessed me by reminding me of my future in You.

My soul is cleaned, cleared, and sanctified. It never has to hide, but now can abide. My physical nature has fought the wars, but my true reality lies within. The outer me would strut in every worldly rut, but my soul was patiently waiting for me to reveal Your goodness within.

In the quiet and stillness of the birds of the air and the trees on the ground, all the world reveals Your grandeur. So it's time for the yell to be noticed in this world . . . a quell to BE just who You are in them and me. In stillness!

Amen.

April 5

Lord, allow me to see what is true, real, and beautiful, for all these things are gifts from You. Any less creates in me the blues, but it dissolves as everything is controlled by You.

Your call is never-ending. As I look to You, I never stall, for it draws me near to Your light, erasing the darkest night.

Surrounded by Your spirit lifts me and fills me with Your love from above. Reveal the perfection of Your creation to me today.

Amen!

April 6

My heart is open, my mind is pure, and my soul receives Your guidance clearly and so dearly.

When I let go of the world of my own creation, I receive joy as if I were a young boy.

My false fear fades with Your protection, and I reject all that's lesser than me, which brings a new serenity.

So I am whole, and my light is no longer behind the bushel. For Your glory abounds where it was always to be found.

Amen.

April: God's Beautiful Creation

April 7

May I increase my awareness so I can receive You. The valley of confusion is healed in Your truth, enabling me to thrive in spirit. I no longer receive life's demerits, as You are my increasing priority. I lose judgment and confusion and discover a glimpse of the beauty of unity.

May I pursue what makes me come alive as my spirit learns to thrive.

Amen!

April 8

I approach Your throne of grace, Lord, with confidence of receiving Your mercy. For this is a place to grow and know that You created me.

No matter what I go through, I walk with You. You call me to carry on, and I have no fear that I might fall because, after all, You are God, and I am Yours. Creator and created.

Every morning, You restore me before my feet even hit the floor. As I fully comprehend Your majesty, Your miracles expand my mind, and I can't find anything that compares to You. I delight in being created by You, my creator, sustainer, and friend.

Amen!

April 9

Lord, judge me not for who I am but for who You are within me.

    May I have this same vision in those I meet: that you are with them, too. We are all an expression of You, our creator, designer, and Father.

    When all I have to do is receive what You always planned for me, I am free of worldly complications and can trust in Your everlasting protection of unspeakable love.

Amen!

April 10

Remind me when I pass a stranger on the street today that with an open heart and smiling face, I can reveal You. May I recognize You within them as their smile unleashes You, which I need to see. It's in the briefest encounters with strangers in the street that I get to meet and greet the light of the world that is within. My hope is You, and I see it and reveal it from within. I need not be solemn but awake and simply look around—it's You in every color, shape, and space.

That's how every one of my frowns gets turned upside down, as the fuel of my soul's engine is You.

Amen

April 11

The Heavens declare Your glory and the sky Your handiwork.
This power and glory pull me through. Life's journey can confuse me, so I often lose this Heavenly perspective. I lift my eyes to see the glory to be above the sky as the true power to carry on is Your energy in me.

Your wonders of the world, as magnificent as they are, fail to expand beyond the simple truth this very hour that my core is Your shiniest star.

This reality magnifies all the stars in the galaxy. The wonders for the whole world to see are but faint compared to You within me. You allow me to come alive and generate energy driven by the greatest miracle You gave to me—my life just as I was meant to be.

So, when I'm sad, glad, or just following some short-term fad, I always have the hope to be truly joyful, for anchoring me is Your truth and reality within.

Amen!

April 12

Every good gift is from my Father above, coming down from Heavenly lights for all nights. My mind's emotions are no longer fleeting when grounded in the promises of my Father, and to Him, I'm no bother. I wait upon thee, and in this, I can be free and rest to pass any test.

But in the moment, I can forget and get in a stir as the whirl of the world can seemingly unfurl. However, in that moment, I remember just whose I am as that's who I was always meant to be. You, my savior, comfort me like I'm a baby, innocent and vulnerable without You.

In my brokenness, the seed of my transformation grows. For grief and joy are sisters raising me higher as I trust confidently in the Holy Spirit within me. Glee will never truly flee as I accept and love the way I was meant to be, which is totally free!

Amen!

_____
_____
_____
_____
_____
_____
_____
_____
_____

April: God's Beautiful Creation

April 13

I am enough! I have enough! When I deeply know this truth, I know who God naturally created me to be, and I can fully celebrate. Stop reaching and start accepting. Stop desiring and start receiving the fullness of His presence within. This light never ceases. Receive Your greatest gift, you and me, just as we are with the gifts He has created for us.

For He eliminates fear, guilt, shame, and separation. I was created for the beauty of life, the richness of fellowship, His promise of abundance, the joy of harmony, and for His full delight.

Amen!

April 14

I see joy in the moment and know God's grace. I receive the laughter and love of the people of God that surround me. I have a love for all things and feel the peace that's the gift of my Lord. Even the challenges are met with His grace and peace through the journey. I receive this truth as it's the inheritance of our earthly presence. This gift is from our creator, sustainer, and savior.

So be it for me and for You from Him!

April 15

I am renewed and refreshed with the assurance of the Lord's love. The day is met with the hope of His promises and the opportunity to be hope and encouragement to those I meet today. May I be awakened to God's goodness in the miracles and reminders of the simple beauties I often forget to rejoice in.

May I be reminded of His grace by the rising of the sun, the taste of breakfast, the comfort of my pets, and the camaraderie of His people. May I see the smile of the Lord in the child I see pass by. May the simple truth of His goodness and love be seen by me, and may His grace and love be on my face to all I encounter.

May we see Him in all His creation and created today!

Amen

April 16

Lord of love, lead, guide, surround, and immerse me in Your grace, peace, and love today. May I turn the frowns around that I encounter. May I meet people and see You in them. Lead me to Your purposes and see that every challenge I confront becomes growth in faith, the strength to provide peace to the powerless, comfort to the broken, courage to the fearful.

I'm Yours, and Your permanent presence provides Your warmth through me. May I encounter You by being with Your children today, and may I equally be comforted by them as I experience Your unity through my humility.

May I walk my path today with the confident assurance that Your purpose guides each step I take.

Amen!

April: God's Beautiful Creation

April 17

Through my loss, I am nearer to the heart of God. Part of my soul is with those who are with Him, as God created ME and THEM for this specific purpose: to love one another just as God loves me. We are called to know, share, feel, and live this truth both on Heaven and Earth. Those in Heaven are needed to be God's energy of love, and until we're called to unity with them, we are God's very love and their spirits here.

I can see Heaven's gate in my dreams, and it has a welcome mat for me! I don't have to earn it; everything has already been done. My soul was created to know this in both Heaven and Earth. Those I've loved dearest here are there, waiting for me to arrive at the party of harmony for eternity. Unspeakable joy, indescribable union. Struggling immediately melts to celebration.

Until then, while we're here, the only real job I have is to know and share this love. The rest was just an excuse to meet You and share that Heaven's Gate has a welcome mat for both me and You!

Amen, my brothers and sisters on earth and in Heaven!

_____
_____
_____
_____
_____
_____
_____
_____

April 18

God of abundance, take my scarcity away. Lord, awake me to the deceit of my fears to clearly see the strength I have in You. May my courage be in the truth of who You created me to be. I desire to not shy away from vulnerability, for it gives me a common bond of reality with others.

Replace all worry with a fearless faith in You that renews me every morning. May I awake today with no doubt that I am Yours and You are mine. In this truth, there is only abundance, grace, and wholeness. In this truth, I am enough; I have enough.

Your plans are perfect for me today to conquer all fears and meet every challenge. In this, even my grief melts to hope as I trust that ALL Your ways are for my good. May I be an example of Your loving kindness. As I embrace You more fully, help me to be strength for those You have given me to know and love.

Take from me the deceit that steals through the worldly practices of comparing, separating, and winning. Instead, fill me with a pure desire for unity, peace, and seeing all others as equals because I see You in them, and may they see You in me.

Allow Your abundance to erase any lie that I am not enough, as I am perfect from Your lens. May Your love and abundance abound and be the rallying cry to humanity.

Amen!

_____
_____
_____
_____

April 19

This is the day the Lord has made; I will rejoice and be glad in it!

I am delighted in who He has made me to be, for it is by His perfect design.

I wake to gratefully celebrate the lessons of life, the struggles that strengthen me, and the challenges that make me wiser. Thank You for the love within me and every person You gave me to know. Family, friends, and the familiar faces I see—each is a reminder of Your endless goodness to me.

The sight of a bird, the shade of a tree, all of nature brings Your joy to me.

God, thank You for You, the God that You are, the creator of my soul, and the hope I have in You.

Amen!

April 20

Nature's call is Your voice, my Lord. The beauty You extend is also within. The bird of the air's magnificence is equal to the vitality of the vision You have gifted to me.

The roots that ground a tree are as deep as its outward height, just as the depth of my spirit grounds my being.

The power of the flow of the river of life guides the direction of my path entrusted to You.

May my vision have spiritual clarity, my soul know peace, and my trust in You grow more confident daily.

Amen!

April 21

Lord my God, awaken my soul to delight in the presence of others. Use me to be Your very own encouraging love. May the illusions of being less than You created me to give way to the truth of Your perfect love. There is only delight in You, my God, for my soul. If You can see the light in me, it can never be dimmed. My delight is in You as You placed the joy of Your light in me. The light of life of Your creation is the center of my being. Remind me when I'm discouraged who I am in You.

Amen!

April 22

Lord, allow me to be still enough to see Your wholeness in this fast-paced world. You speak into my heart most profoundly when I remain still.

Slow my steps to feel the ground of Your creation. May it anchor me to Your promises. Allow me to discern Your guidance. Allow me to commune quietly with all of Your children in Your gift of nature. May I learn more than I attempt to instruct or teach. May I unlearn all that leaves me short of Your perfection of love.

Allow me to glimpse Your eternal plan that breaks the temporal pursuits that can consume my day. May I grow in the confidence of who I am in You! Allow me to see the kindness I can extend to the comfort of my friends, not because of anything I can do as I am sinful, but when surrendered to You, I learn and relearn that resistance to surrender is the needless cause of my suffering. I can be used by You who is holy, perfect, and righteous!

Amen!

April 23

Allow me to become still. May the ability to develop my spirit to rest in You bring seeds of wisdom that erase this fear. I no longer fear but instead thirst for Your serenity. As I quiet my heart and just listen, Your spirit unfolds within me. Your guidance and wisdom have been waiting for me to learn this mastery of the grace I only find when I'm alone.

For I have feared time alone with just my Father and me, but why? It prevented me from seeing the stillness of the night and the majesty of natural beauties You created to share with me, just You, the inventor, and me, Your invented.

The distractions of the world deceive, as the greatest deception is self-deception.

May I learn to grow wise through the solemn times when I feared being alone. Might I grow in spirit to see You most clearly and desire You most dearly. This is the time I get to hear You and just sit in Your lap. Just me and You, as I learn on earth even before I'm in Heaven, to be one in You alone.

Amen.

_____
_____
_____
_____
_____
_____
_____
_____
_____
_____

April 24

I awake in the morning, and in the rising of the sun, I am reminded of Your magnificence. God's glory envelopes me with the goodness of His grace. As the day progresses, the unfolding of His mysteries reveals the greatness of God's gifts. On the mountain peak, You call to me; on the ocean's shore, You embrace me; in the valley, You hold me near and whisper in my ear. For You are most dear when my heart is open and near You as the rays of Your light illuminate my soul.

   I am made whole as I am in You and You in me.

Amen!

April 25

God, give Your love through me to Your children. Then I become a conveyor of Your light, and I delight. As I take the tour of life that You inspired, I fully discover who You say I am. I know I am all right because it was due to Your design of man that I am the model, make, and mark that I AM! You are my author, engineer, architect, and florist!

I now receive the delight of Your energy, so my euphoria from Your design shines within.

There once was a thorn in my side, but it's been released, and it lets the light of healing in. Where there was once darkness hiding from man, there is light of God within.

I no longer fear the illusions of the commands of man, but I fully receive, know, and now comprehend the light of love of my creator for the purity and goodness that reflects His perfection of grace within my original existence.

I am who You made without fail, flaw, or even imperfection. No man's opinion ever truly mattered, inhibited, or could keep me from becoming You in me, and ME in You fully blossomed!

Amen!

April 26

"You alone are the LORD. You made the Heavens, even the highest heavens, and all their starry host, the earth and all that is on it, the seas and all that is in them. You give life to everything, and the multitudes of heaven worship You." — Nehemiah 9:6

Why don't I simply accept my brothers, sisters, sons, and daughters the way You have made them and delight in what You did just as I radiantly accept the sun, moon, and stars?

Yet I struggle to receive Your beauty in the created.

The creation is easy to see Your perfection in the distance, but Your created is right here up close next to me.

I never look to the skies and see Your "mistakes," but in Your created, it's a struggle. So it's Your most complicated design that has all the flaws?

It's my struggle until it's my surrender. When it's my surrender, it's acceptance, delight, and love as they are a piece of You that is just like the piece in me.

What we as humans see as imperfections or disappointments and even embarrassments are God's perfections . . . if I could only see and accept them as gifts.

We're so quick to see others as broken, imperfect, or a victim of tragedy or special needs to the world's view.

Each is not flawed but fantastic, not unfortunate but radically blessed, an opportunity to see Your deepest love in each of Your created just as Your creation. If it's perfect by Your design, it's great for the eyes of my heart. May I see from within that's Your perfect love in me to see Your beauty in the one before me.

After all, it's my brother and me!

Amen.

April: God's Beautiful Creation

April 27

God in me is the hope I have. He gives me the love within to look for the good in everyone. When I look for that, I find God in them and in me.

When I no longer try to change the one before me, I delight in who He made them and me to be. No tree ever has annoyed me or made me think, "Wow, that branch is a little too fat or thin."

It's simply perfection in God's creation and plan, just like the one before me. Now, I see from an open heart rather than the hardness of my head.

Indeed, this is the gift of this life. May I not miss it.

May I receive it and see it in process in God's perfect plan! What is meant to be by His Will will always be!

Amen!

April 28

Practicing radical kindness to those I've struggled with most offers the greatest healings in my soul to grow the muscle of God's own love within.

May God give me the patience and resolve to practice this.

He has said in Him we are a new creation. May I be a new creation in this way, reflecting the enduring peace that passes all understanding. May my projection become my Lord's reality in me.

Lord, may my frustration dissipate in this deep kindness that is forged in the crucible of selfless love You designed, defined, and perpetuated.

Amen!

April 29

May my day be filled with blessing, surrounded by God's light, highlighted with laughter and cheer.

May my heart be kept open and lead my spirit to the presence of joy. I am with You this day, Lord, and always!

You assure me that You never depart from me. Help me to sustain these truths and understandings that extinguish all doubt and fear.

In the warmth of Your presence, I do not tire. In my eyesight, I have total clarity when I am resting in You, as my wandering mind ceases, and the perfection of Your harmony beats in my soul. Lord, make me Your instrument of music that delights within my heart and those I come to be with and know today!

Amen!

April 30

Lord, give me the strength of wisdom to hold loosely to what I have and think I am.

May my illusions of the perception of others give way to the fullness of the magnificence I already am in You.

The false illusions and the opinions of others corrupt the soul and minimize my joy.

But when I see through the clouds and the darkness of man, the day of the breakthrough of the glory of God is breathtaking to behold. So I'll remain still in fullness of Your presence within and gasp in delight.

Stunned and amazed, I now see the birds of the air and the glory of the fins of the fish in the sea, but equally beautiful is Your very own breath in me. My Lord, You have given me everything, and only the world within created a blindness to the fullness of Your beauty to unfold in the gifts of nature where my eyes can begin a new focus upon the glory beyond. The foretaste of Heaven is all around and has always been; You've just been waiting for my eyes like a baby's at first sight to awaken and take in the glory You unfold.

God, may I greet Your glory on this day as I see higher and farther because the focus of the lens of my eye reveals the promised glory of Heaven for which I was initially created. Thank You, Father, for I have always been home in the backyard, and You were just waiting for me to come knocking at the front door to behold the fullness of the glory for which I was always in store.

Amen!

Whispers From Heaven

MAY: SURRENDER

May: Surrender

May 1

Lord, guard my thoughts. The quality of my life depends upon my thoughts. So, Lord, I call out to You to ask You to guard, control, and take control of my mind. It's not to be a land mine but can be a tool of the divine. I ask You to create in me every divine thought through thee. When it goes off half-cocked and in circular thoughts, I manufacture misery, a disease that can be cured by a fresh breeze.

I am not a zombie. As I gaze and awaken from the haze, I can change the station to Your serenity that comes with the wisdom of the thought. At times, I don't even know how it stops. It's an automatic drive until I awake and realize I do not have to be paralyzed.

So, I ask that You would create purification in my mind to create the finest possibility. Thoughts of hope are the perfect cure for a dope. I surrender because You are my best friend.

Amen!

May 2

Lord, replace my frustrated yelling with Your whispers of love. Without anger, I am free to embrace Your greetings of peace. I feel Your serenity when I lose my selfish tendencies, allowing me to grow in trust (an absolute must) and be rooted in Your design.

It becomes my mantra to let go of my own desires and use those now empty hands to embrace the grace You freely give. I open my heart to the warmth of Your love and focus on You, my very best friend.

Amen!

May: Surrender

May 3

Awareness, acceptance, and understanding bring peace, banishing the deceptions that block me from surrendering to Your shield of protection. You are not flipping a spiritual coin to determine my emotions or fate; Your plan for me is certain, secure, and safe.

I simply need to be sure I am trusting You. As I do, I let go and stop resisting Your perfect plan.

Amen!

May 4

In my Youth, I absorbed what I observed in my greater community.

I was taught that a man's ultimate identity is in being a provider. Perhaps this is how the world once kept score, but that is a bore. I learned that I am SO MUCH MORE!

The meaning of life and my manhood rests in what it always did before I understood.

Lord God, I stand here and declare all things come from You! To earn some credit before others is a waste of my greatest gift: to be a reflection of Your love! I must love freely in all circumstances and be a reflection of your light!

I'm aware and awake and can attest that You can turn my valleys into mountain peaks, but it requires perseverance and growing trust in You. As I walk this part of the path, I surrender regret, for my growing trust is in You, Lord.

Amen.

May: Surrender

May 5

May my purpose come from leading a purposeful life. For the gift of life You granted to me was never to be drudgery or intermittent tragedy.

May my heart remain open so my soul can smile. When this is all I know, I can serve and bestow here below. Then my circumstances unfold just as You foretold. But when my heart is closed, it blocks the flow of Heaven's glow. Beware of the ego's deceptive flight. Fueled by delight, it masquerades as my true self, leading me astray.

To be free of this neurotic mystery, all I must do is surrender and awaken to the truth of Your power this very hour.

For in this, I suffer less and experience Your serenity.

Now, my experience is NOT intermittent euphoria. Neurotics fake "happiness" to satisfy my ego, which leads to depression and anxiety. But when I rest my soul in You, this falsehood disappears. Truth has tamed the obsessive behavior in me; I am free, healed by my journey within.

Every experience is meant for me to depend and draw upon Your spirit in me. I am now awake and serene, steady through both calm and stormy waters. I'm now in my true form, where serenity in its perpetual stability never deceives me.

Amen!

_____
_____
_____
_____

May 6

You are the source of grace. In resting in trust and surrendering control, my soul is balanced. I am learning to let go of the illusion of control. Why do I fight to hold on and create misery? Then I'm releasing negativity, and I renew myself in your inspired positivity.

With glee, I do not carry what does not belong to me. You restore me with comfort, confidence, and an open heart, which aligns my mind with you. My trust grows, fighting fear that is only falsely near. The days unfold just as you foretold for my good and your glory. The wisdom and assurance I gain is your gift I need to just embrace. Indeed, your grace covers this place.

Amen.

May: Surrender

May 7

Lord, I have three levels to my mind; may I experience all three levels in all realities. You go before me, unfolding peace that is coming. These three facets are the conscious mind, the subconscious mind, and the unconscious mind, which are proof of Your wonders within.

An ordered conscious mind allows the subconscious mind to solve my problems, for this allows me knowledge over ignorance, good over evil, and light over all.

It's only when I get lazy and allow the mind to be in self-drive that I no longer thrive and am driven by the jive of the unconscious. Left in control, it leads as though it has my needs ordered, but it causes mental bleeds from the weeds of the mind, making me consciously blind. Without a compass, I am lost in this confusion, whose illusion leads to the wrong conclusion. In this, I realize what You intended for me. When I awake and look around, I see my Father in Heaven revived my consciousness to arouse my soul!

The valley of unconsciousness is lost to the mountain peaks of consciousness. The heart was the one always right and relieving all fright. Your light is Your very reflection from the start, so I fully take heart in Your light!

Amen!

_____
_____
_____
_____
_____

May 8

Today, I awake and simply ask, wait, and listen. What is Your will for me today? Guide me as on a slide to Your unfolding purpose. May You speak *to* me and *through* me. I open my heart from the day's start to simply ask where I should go, who I can encourage, where I can grow, and how I can know Your love so it overflows.

Everything that grows from within is a gift that knows from whom my love shows. There is no guessing when I'm receiving and simply believing. You are within me.

Amen.

May 9

May the light of my Lord lift my heart. Call me nearer to You. Free me of the world's worries to know Heaven's promises of peace. Lighten my load, Lord, leading me Heavenward. Your truths melt my fears; Your promises provide peace; Your realities erase my worry.

May I live today as a new creation, my burdens lighter, my peace purer, freeing me of anything that separates me from You, my Lord, Your children, and the gifts of Your creation.

Amen.

May 10

God of creation and Lord of my reality, You alone created my very existence.

Use me, God, to be Your co-creator, not just a spectator. Put Your active workmanship in the lives I touch, the creation I behold, and the animals I love. I'll live by the breath of Your spirit on this earth until I am with You, not only in spirit but in reality and truth.

May I live expectantly for this promise I have in You! Make my life a divine expression of Your goodness.

Amen and Amen and Amen!

May 11

God's clarity is in the simplicity of His message. God's power in my heart is my will to trust Him. His absolute love is the compass for my path. I am never lost because He is in my heart with no difficulty to understand. It's not complex to trust and love. How hard is that to do? What rules my way is all found in these two simple words: Love and Trust, which is all the truth I need.

Amen!

May 12

Lord, I trust in You. Thank You for the uplifting of the power of prayer to heal, guide, and direct. The power is from You alone.

Nothing depends upon me; I just need to trust You.

As I face difficulty, possibilities of comfort simply rest in turning to and trusting You.

I am filled with strength that defeats my weaknesses. The courage awaits me that quashes fear as all I have to do is trust You and surrender to You in prayer.

May I not worry or become weary as You Yourself remind me to run to You in humility and to simply trust and talk to You.

So, I ask that You greet me this morning to turn my frown around and trust truly in the power of prayer.

In that trust, I ask for You to mend my heart that hurts for myself and those who know struggle from the wounds of life, revealing the lessons to my walk, perfecting my trust in You.

Amen!

May 13

My Lord, may the FOMO (Fear of missing out) in me give way to JOLA (Joy of living authentically). I am but in process of living, failing, learning, and growing. You, my God, are always there as the breath in my lungs and the power in my step.

God's spirit in me leads and sustains. As I grow in grace, I receive peace and forgiveness, recognizing that what I saw as attacks were lessons from God to love more and stay in the light, drawing me closer to Him, the ultimate source of love. There has been not one second of anger, grief, struggle, or strife wasted, as it all strengthened my being and softened my heart to sand the roughness in my soul to Heavenly perfection. My Heavenly-bound being softens to the perfection within as a butterfly sheds its shell as a caterpillar.

May the warmth of the presence of the Lord lift me to the highest heights of the Heavens as my only eternal plan.

Amen!

May 14

Dear God, I call to You to orient my mind, make my heart soft, and open my ears to receive and trust Your love for me. This transforms doubt into security.

Control the theatre of my mind to rest in Your perfection. When my thoughts are in control, they seed doubt.

Wake me up to Your full presence.

The moment I live in doubt, it fuels the lie that temporarily separates You from me in my mind. You never left my side; then I see You! You always restore me to the overflowing river of Your love, acceptance, and grace.

I rid myself of the lies creating false depression. When I know I'm Yours, when You call me, You allow me the delight of harmony with You.

My wellness is not something I get permission for, nor is it given to me by another. My wellness is the freedom that You, my God, gave me within my soul.

This is when I speak the solo within my soul, which is the freedom found through suffering surrendered with trust in You!

Q. When does suffering stop?
A. When I decide!

Amen.

May: Surrender

May 15

May I live by the spirit; therefore, I will keep in step with the spirit.

May Your spirit be the pull of every step of my walk.

I fought so hard, at first to survive, then to be known, achieving, earning, looking for honor to be worthy in the eyes of others, wanting to make something of myself.

Finally, I surrendered the struggle on the mountaintop of this world. Now, seeing and fully realizing just how pleased You already were with me all along!

It's who You made me to be, I now can see! The haze of ego leads to comparison and the juggernaut of judgment, bringing the poison of separation, which has now melted. The struggle was just to end the fight for You to fully be seen in me.

This reality needs no affirmation or approval of man. Not even from a man, mom, father, or even myself. But by just being who I was born to be by Your intention, needing no approval of any man. The fight is over, and joy has begun.

It brings no fight, flight, or confrontation. But sharing the world, now as a dreamer living in the world as one. I guess it's Heaven on earth.

I no longer have fear, for now I know true faith! I walk in mystery, erasing the walk of misery. It was just all along my choice to make. I now choose true and deep faith without judgment. May You, Lord, be known here by Your love being known in mine.

Amen!

May 16

Lord, awaken my consciousness to be open and free. May I no longer surrender to the mind's cruising, creating the ego's bruising from the illusion of control. The mind's utter pollution disguises as a solution. But when I recognize these falsities, I avoid the fear that was never near.

Comparison creates misery. I have to keep my spirit awake so I can be innocent and free. I now can show this freedom within me. My perfect heart never beats for defeat. All I need is clarity, peace, and freedom of heart between all others and me. Life is not a race for first place but a relay of unity in all earth's community.

For, in this new mindset, I can let the sun's rays warm the ocean's bay, creating a sunny reality.

Judgment and self-condemnation block me from loving others. Why has this been my auto-set? If I let it be and recognize when I'm counting sheep in my sleep, I can awaken to this greater reality. I guess my prejudices are the laziest way for my mind to be polluted by fumes that loom and create false dooms.

This confusion causes delusion. I set my mind on consciousness as I am ready for my heart to play the first part. So now I can let my heart take off like a jet and let all the made-up worry dissolve.

Think, think. How much easier is it to just be? So be it . . . so I will. All I must do is recognize and surrender to awaken consciously. Lord, let me be free of the prison of my mind for the freedom of the heart. After all, that's the original model You created for me. I will surrender to thee and YES . . . I'm now free.

Amen.

May: Surrender

May 17

Holy Spirit, capture my existence and cause a thirst in me, which only can be quenched by You.

May the filling of Your presence illuminate my path.

May my delight be in reflecting You. May Your comfort protect and guide me in such a way that Your presence is felt by the energy I emanate.

Make me a conveyor of Your energy to each of Your children I pass by. Give me eyes to see the wounded spirits who can be lifted by Your presence in me by my eye contact with a passerby. May my smile heal the broken-hearted.

May I have the humility to receive the same and see You within those I meet today.

May I replace judgment with love, condemnation with understanding, and comparison with compassion.

May I be given strength to freely forgive and let go of offenses that create a hard heart, self-focus, and a reactive, egoistic response.

May I respond to slights without fights. May the car behind me that honks not cause volcanic reaction within but the response of a friendly wave. May I not assume the other has wronged me because it is all well in my soul.

When my peace is anchored in You, I forgive rather than be offended. May I see it all as You do from the perch of the eternal, where I can gain the patience to see a Heavenly lesson in my frustration.

May kindness become the strength of my health.

May the filling of Your spirit bring peace from You through me today.

Amen!

May: Surrender

May 18

Gaining insight from our Lord and surrendering the illusion of control brings blessing, peace, and joy.

Lord, free me of the complications of man's creations to freely consume Your natural blessings, bringing elation.

My joy in freedom is unleashed as I surrender the driver's wheel of my life to You. It is no longer I who does anything but You who does everything.

WOW! Why did I have to grow too old and tired to see the simplicity of the freedom of Your indwelling?

You were always there, waiting for me to let go and be exactly who and what You have called me and to enjoy where You have placed me.

May my purpose from You unfold in me on this day, for today is all there is until You do it all over again. Then, there are no worldly constraints of work, survival, success, or competition.

Instead, the energetic joy of just being me from You delights, encourages, and unites me to all others. The rest are not as I contrived, but they each are perfect on their own journey designed by You just as You have done for me.

Count it all as joy, as it's all a gift from You to me. You are ours, and we are Yours!

Amen!

_____
_____
_____
_____
_____

May 19

Oh Lord, spare me irritation, for when I get irritated, it grows into frustration. When I get frustrated, it grows to anger. When it grows to anger, it creates separation. When separation ensues, the feelings of despair and depression consume my emotions and take my mind for a ride in the depths of the dark sea.

Awaken my soul to the stability of the road of diversion You offer me. When irritation is halted at its origin, it creates a holy direction. Irritation fades to peace, and peace creates the foundation for joy in my spirit and a song in my lungs and a dance in my step, leading to unity, harmony, and brotherly love.

During only a split second when I awaken in the morning, I must choose which road to traverse that day.

May I realize the suffering I create in this moment that comes from my imagination. Lord, in that moment, remind me of who You lead and inspire me to be. Transform the irritation to understanding and instead awaken this day to reality that leads me to Heaven's highway.

Amen!

May 20

Lord, the thing I fear is the change that will free me. Allow me to get rid of this fear and trust You more.

The pegs of my tent that bind it to the ground create my attachments, and the illusion of my control prevents healing, growth, peace, and serenity. When the pegs are freed, and the tent's flaps are loosened, the fabric transforms into a hot air balloon filled with Heavenly helium that lifts me to a higher perspective, where I see harmony through the lens of wisdom. This snapshot is Heaven in me, which allows judgment to dissolve, projection to be erased, and separation surrendered to unity.

Free me from the attempted human control of my soul as well as attempts to control others.

They will not learn to walk if I carry them. We will not learn to trust You when I attempt to replace their need for You with myself.

Who cares what's "fair"? Only in loving and surrendering all to full-blown gratitude will this shortcoming cease. This will facilitate my highest use on earth and the greatest good for the full delight of my soul.

These are the pegs that falsely created the illusion of anchoring. I am now joyfully untethered. This deception prevented me from soaring at the heights You called me to.

It's the fear of change that keeps me the same, but in the change is You and who You're calling me to be, revealing Your glory in me. The old patterns and ruts are the veins that are choking the flow of freedom.

The new flow of the river washes me and guides me higher, farther, and for my greatest use of You at work in me. I let go of the attachments that held me in place and the fear that I must confront and go through to bring me home here

May: Surrender

and now. This is what I must do. Bring me to this edge of preparation for my permanent home of Your design.

Lord, give me the strength to be weak enough to let go of the things that hold me back and to simply trust You!!!

Amen!

May 21

Keep my heart open, Lord. May my mind not close the doorway to my soul through my gut. Allow my intuition to rule over my intellect, as my most important intelligence is not artificial. It's allowing the voice that's You in me to be trusted, not tested, and fully explored and never expired. I am alive in You, Lord. When I realize my instinctive steps are Your callings, I understand that I was part of Your intention long before any human took credit for me. Instead of reaching for what I want most, I accept only what I need because my human desires are not all from You. May I not be fooled as it's my mere EGO edging God out. Reveal the part of me whose joy depends knowingly on You as I surrender.

May this strength of spirit overcome ego's deceit.

Darkness dissolves to love, which is God fully revealed in me.

Amen!

May 22

The knower of all. The one who sees all. The one who is both the creation and the creator yet uniquely the creator of my very own being. My God, my fortress, the protector of my soul.

You are in every breath I take. I have all that I am or ever need in You, my Lord. I am enough. I have enough.

I remain still, hopeful, and yearning for the answer to every question I can conceive. You are only far from me when I deceive my soul and give ear to the rumination of my mind.

You know the exact place I will fall, fail, or be weary, and You are ready to catch me.

Your truth and glory unfold before me in every way, every day. Your beauty and magnificence never cease. When I forget to look upon You, I become weary, waiting to be renewed. Just one glance at You makes me whole again, and I am reawakened.

Why do I think in those fleeting moments I can do it alone? But it's Your right to guide my sight, and on You I might alone depend. This reminds me to become wholly renewed by looking up at You, my king, creator, and friend. It's You in me who makes me always on the mend.

Amen!

May 23

"For it is God who works in You, both to will and to work for His good pleasure." Philippians 2:13 (ESV)

This, my Lord, is a promise You gave to me, yet my emotions change, and circumstances, opinions, and perspectives do as well. The world and our nation that surrounds me often confuse me.

I forget the promise of Your unchanging, constant goodness.

My anchor of attachment to the reality of this world hinders me. This is where I'm fully present. The lessons are limited by my ability to understand. In its chaos, torment, confrontation, and confusion of warring hostilities, I forgot to simply trust You.

Nothing catches You by surprise. No one is outside of Your control, as Your will includes both active and permissive will. Therefore, nothing is a surprise to You. Yet, it is constant to me. I guess it's okay if I don't know, but You do.

So let me know what I should know and just rest with it all left to You.

Release me of my human need to control or even understand, as it's all a part of Your perfect plan. May I trust it to You to will, direct, and pursue.

I am here, Lord, available and Yours. Use me in any way You choose.

The only thing I need to do is be ready for You to holler out to me to come home. Because Lord, my heart has a longing to be at home, knowing You have already picked the time and place for my Heavenly home.

Until then, I will be listening for Your calls and entering each day in trust that it will unfold as You ordered. With my deepest love and longing, my Lord, God, Father, King, and friend: Use me!

Amen!

May 24

God, when I awaken, remind me to greet and welcome my heart. My head is already awakened; that's "who" got me up. Now, awaken my heart, full bloom and open, because that decision is up to me until I am fully surrendered to thee.

My head wants to be left in dictatorial control. It will be until my heart awakens to take its place. Then love again is in control. You, God, are in control in me, not my headspace.

As You alone command that place!

Amen!

May: Surrender

May 25

Resting in my Lord, I know I can be a calm river beneath any storm. When I rest in my inner life, choreographed by God, there is only perpetual peace, void of suffering. Changing emotions are a mere illusion that the truth of God's love is unchanging and independent, therefore consistent in any circumstance. Then, I no longer swing on the pendulum from happy to sad.

There is now no external unpleasantness that disturbs the inner peace that is God's gift to me. When I approach life's challenges with this confidence-fueling neutrality, there is only satisfaction. I merely need to trust and rest in Him.

So be it, for in Him is the promise of this strength of truth.

Amen!

May 26

Lord, take from me that which prevents me from the fruits of Your own spirit.

May love and a desire for peace grow from the void of those things that have overtaken me, drawing me away from this joy You created me for.

I know there is no power greater than You in me, so no one can take me from these great blessings of life and love.

May I not be pulled away by fear but drawn by desire to be like You rather than to please others to fit in. May I know I have all I ever needed to be fully lifted by the truth of the presence of Your spirit in my soul.

I often conform to lesser things in a desire to be noticed, worthy, or simply just to be seen on this world's stage.

May my practice become You in me without words but simply a peace that brings light of Your love through me.

Amen!

May 27

Lord, I pray for compassion that leads my heart and the hearts of mankind.

Maybe tomorrow, I will understand today. For my confusion is knowing the peace that comes from You and yet seeing the division, confrontation, and disharmony that leads to separation of the souls You breathed to life on earth.

I rest, trust, and know that You alone can bring the stillness that provides the peace and love You authored for my heart and the hearts for Your children.

Might my ego's desire to be "right" give way to Your path of peace for this nation and world.

May Your breath in me awaken and oxygenate my heart to see how I can bring harmony to those I commune with today.

May this deep desire become the contagion that overcomes this world and becomes Your love revealed in us, here and now.

Amen!

May 28

Lord, thanks for the wisdom I don't readily recognize from You, but as the oats are on the ground for the goats to feed, so is Your wisdom to nourish my soul.

As I discovered "I," I clenched to it . . . to be SOMEBODY. Then, I discovered "mine," and I became attached and held onto it to show my WORTH to the world. Then I learned both are YOURS, and I found FREEDOM in You!

I am now gladly being just Yours. Therefore, I am always enough, and I always have enough!

Your love is like the wind. I can't see it, but I feel it! It allows me to fly so high, and all I ever needed to do was to surrender to You! So simple but yet so hard that I couldn't understand it until nearly the end. What a perfect journey.

Amen!

May 29

Thank You, Lord, for all that's ever been.

I see now it was all a lesson for me to grow to trust in You!

To lose the ridiculousness that I could ever know or be anything apart from You. My stillness in spirit was developed and forged in the disguise of the miseries of life to know the sweetness of You! You fill my inner being.

All of life, I focused as though the shell was significant, only to experience that the pain of each crack of the exterior would bring me to an unimaginable peace in You in the interior. You placed and set forth every hour and every detail of my life's existence for me to bloom into Your grace of love in this space and time.

Perhaps if it had not been so difficult, I would have had to wait to be with You to see You.

But my haze has been lifted by the difficulty of life in Your goodness.

I can bring myself to thank You for the experiences that led me to this space and time.

My deepest betrayal lasted only a portion of a day, yet the pain of my ego attached to it for years.

The grief of death in my life revealed the most precious loss I could know, but now it's the spirit in me that reveals You in me.

Love takes time to grow, know, and be!

So be it!

Amen!

_____
_____
_____

May 30

God, increase in me the emotions that magnify happiness and quiet those that cause suffering.

Free me of all obsessions as it is the addiction to my suffering.

Free me of the need to perform or please another, as it only builds walls of separation. In separation, there is no unity; therefore, harmony cannot exist.

Replace this illusion and deceit of performance with freedom of spirit in who You created me to be as a reflection of You. When I truly know this, I no longer fret of being worthy because it's You in me who will then be seen.

May my spirit invite holiness, happiness, and peace.

Only freedom of desire leads to obsession that distorts, steals, and deceives You from being seen in me.

This is my physical nature, devoid of the natural beauty of my spiritual nature. It's You in me, oh God, that is the source of the energy that generates happiness within and receives it from my brothers and sisters and cycles it in return.

May Your spirit in and through me be a lamp to my own heart and a beacon to others.

May I become Your peace offering in pursuit of freedom from suffering and a presence of happiness.

Amen.

May: Surrender

May 31

Oh Lord, my God, create a conviction of compassion within my soul.

May I have knowledge of heart that it is only if others see You in me that I am living a life worthy of who You created me to be.

In this reality, may I obsess over what is fair, responsible, or even will be generous and inspire graciousness, honor, and kindness, for it is my heart's desire to genuinely be these things. But it is all a gift from You through me that I can only bring to offer. In time, I will comprehend why my exact purpose and place in each time and space was for the circumstances I have been in this place.

So often, the poisons of comparison and fairness create scales in my mind of worthiness.

Forgive me when I expect anything in return, even a thank You as whatever grace or kindness I could ever extend to anyone is, was, and will be only from You to me to them all along.

This world confused the heart with the mind and changing emotions that corrupt the beauty of just who You made me to be.

It's so easy to ponder fairness and receive what I am worth, for what is my value apart from You to anyone.

So may I claim this new way of living in which this question resets my course in a moment of decision, frustration, reward, or revenge. As this is what I now must do when these moments occur. May I, Lord, just ask this question in each future moment: What would free and feed my soul?

Amen!

Whispers From Heaven

JUNE: GRATITUDE

June 1

Forgive me, Lord. I know my efforts to be "worthy" cause me to be lesser than you made me to be. Fear brought me here, where I lost my mind so many times. But I find it's better to be kind to others and to myself.

I am grateful for the newfound perspective you grow in me. I open my heart with a fresh start to self-compassion and the freedom of God's love.

I'm no longer afraid to be the real me who is kind all the time. I'm free to release the past and embrace the positivity out there for me. I have God down deep inside of me, fueling permanent joy in my heart!

Amen!

June 2

This is the day that Reid went home to truly know the purity of Your love.

I'm not waiting for You there. You're right here walking beside me. You remind me every new day.

Yet I forget that Your comfort and protection are available to me every day!

The more I experience and trust and lean on You, the more You reveal to me this simplicity that I make so hard: to just be.

I often ask myself, "Just what are You up to?" But the answer lies inside of me: You win, love wins, and I win when I stop fighting and simply trust You. So why do I rebel against the peace You provide and instead let my struggles overwhelm me until I rediscover to rest, carry on, and just BE!

Amen.

June: Gratitude

June 3

All my regrets are anchors to my past wounds, so I release them to You. Lord, allow me to see my ego's grandiosity and replace it with Your grandeur that's already inside of me. This is what You meant for me.

I am free to receive the new view, which acknowledges You as the glue to repair my soul.

I see You more clearly each day as I walk in Your love.

My fears have been overcome, staying in the past so I can rest in peace. So, Lord, give this possibility of renewal that keeps me from the blues. But it's for me to lose the weight I've pulled around, to walk upon the new fertile ground. I stand in awe of my heightened reality.

I'm accepting and believing what I can now see. You freely open the doors to this new beauty. With gratitude for Your grandeur, my Lord—for You're in my heart.

Amen.

June 4

It's in the slightest recesses of my mind that I find the answers to Your mysteries.

For life is a joy when I don't destroy my view of the miracle of You.

When I have clarity, I see just who You are in me. When I do, I comprehend and experience tranquility. The busier I was, I saw only me. Now, I make an effort to be on Your time and see Your glory all around me. I now know Your glow. The more important I thought I was, the less of You I experienced and knew. So, Lord, the contest now for me is to learn to love, as You're filling me with renewed energy.

Amen.

June: Gratitude

June 5

Remove the anger from my soul as a small spark can set an inferno of fire.

May I see that the power found in submitting to Your love can sustain me through any trial of denial.

As I judge so quickly, allow me to see the wound in the one who offends me so they can be healed by brotherly love in and through me. Then they, in return, heal the wound in me, and I, too, am free. I can be grateful to them, seeing their soul as a friend instead of an enemy.

May I freely forgive—for You have forgiven me for so, so much. Collecting animosity is no earthly jewel but only poison to hold on to for no reason for a very long season.

So, especially when it makes no sense, and I'm bent to grievance, set my clenched hands free in forgiveness. For love and hate originate in my heart. May I love from the start so that hate is never my mate. Your love is my ultimate fate.

Amen.

June 6

Greater things than this shall I do—that's what You lead me to.
    Strength and wisdom are my guide. My intuition is God's voice inside . . . may it dissolve my selfish pride and raise the tide. So I hold on for the ride!
    I have a brand new view, for I see now that I'm free. I was searching endlessly for You, but I never looked in the right place. Your spirit was not just waiting for me at the doors of the church one day a week. It's there every day, always ready to speak.
    Only this discovery can bring wholeness and harmony.
    So now I meditate to still my mind, sedate mental troubles, and receive the dopamine without a hangover. Why did I wait so long to calm my soul with Your guidance?
    I am grateful that I no longer have to just bear life's challenges but can see it all as lessons of peace with an eternal lease.

Amen!

June: Gratitude

June 7

Every moment that passes, Lord, is so that I could grow in the strength of You.

I am grateful for all the good things in my life.

I will expand my capacity every day to love You and love others. Each challenge and each obstruction or disappointment is to grow in trust of You. To grow my muscle of faith that causes me to feel connected to You, making me whole and complete.

In this, I know joyfulness as You are the author and creator of joy.

I am content in this moment in Your presence. My hope and confidence are in You, causing life to have less strife as I've cut it with Your knife of perspective so Your love flows freely. The stuff of strife I've held onto was just a false reason to feel blue. All things that were less than they could be are my greatest lessons of wisdom and growth, so my regrets dissolve in the face of moments that built my wisdom. So, as I let go of all that burdens me, I feel uplifted by Your truth.

Amen!

June 8

Lord, give me eyes to see more than my ego needs to be seen.
Free me of the harm I've caused as it's all forgiven sin. You have placed it in the trash bin.
Not only do I ask that I be free of the judgment of others, lift me out of any fear of being judged. For Your love is no longer in doubt so what is all that judgment about? It's the deceit of a mind lesser than me that You never desired for me. May I just move past the doubt that's never been a reality.
May my faith encourage and nurture my own soul to be an abundance of beauty for others. My faith becomes so real by the love I exhibit and naturally share, and am able to bear all within. So hold me, Lord, for You are my prince of peace. No matter what's in store, may I be a light in the path for others to see.
I battle a war between guilt and grace, but You have already won that race. I'm living proof of the victory of Your giving grace.
Thank You for my victory! My faith is not a gold medal to wear but a loving heart to bear.
For no one can free me to be what You planned . . . no one but ME!

Amen.

_____
_____
_____
_____

June 9

The goodness of God is meant to be. His gladness is vast and fills the air.

It is so powerful and clear; it erases all fear. Doubt and worry dissolve with the first ring of His call. So I gaze upon Heaven and breathe in, grazing in the pasture of peace.

I find perpetual serenity when my mind comes completely still with no need other than You.

Amen!

June 10

God of all! Everything that has been and is yet to be is Yours, from the fall to the fiery ball on the horizon. There are no mistakes or happenstances. I look in Your book, which has already told what is yet to unfold.

Your miracles turn my earthly struggles into strength, guiding me along the unique path You created, teaching me to trust Your love from above.

Thank You for all the circumstances of my life that taught me to walk near You, even the grief, betrayal, disappointments, and fear. All of it has been with an eternity in mind, not just this short walk in real-time.

So, with this in mind, my eyes are open to the path You have created just for me. My unique story prepares me for eternal glory.

Amen!

June: Gratitude

June 11

"You who is in me is greater than he who is in the world."
1 John 4:4

When I experience the truth of Your promise, I can let go of the things that created false fear, thinking that trouble was near. But to be free is simply to look through Your eyes and see what I feared was never real.

I place my mind on the beautiful things I find and realize when I'm kind; there is a new glow on the horizon.

The nature of Your creation is to surround me, waking me up to the beauty of this new day.

I open my heart, quiet my mind, and look to Heaven to say, "Thank You, God, for this new day!"

Amen.

June 12

May I expect nothing and be grateful for everything. For when I am awake, I can delight in the simplicity of feeling another's spirit beside me. The less I hide from false pride, the more Your positive energy shines within me.

I do not need a circus act to sedate the disturbances of the world. My body's energy is my outer protection from the world's insurrection, so the chaos I see won't eternally be. My relief from grief is in the belief in serenity, which was always here waiting for me.

My soul is free to be that which God created for me to be, the internal light through any trying night, never overcome by the darkness of the world.

As I have been told in Luke 12:37 (ESV), "Blessed are those servants whom the master finds awake when He comes."

I am awake and alive, and my songs of praise fight away the blues. My eternal future is bright, so I can persevere. I'm reflective and filled with eternal perspective, never focusing on one night but, instead, with eyes fixed on eternity with You.

Amen!

June 13

Lord, You are good. You are good to me in so many ways. You call to me in every way. In every waking hour, You assure me I'm going the right way. In my sleeping hours, You nourish and bless, dissolving the illusions of a mess. My problems are less when I carry them to Thee.

For in Your perfect plan, it's never bland, as I always land where You have directed me. I now stand strong in the land that You gave me to be Your flair in spirit everywhere. As I fully take in this breath, I am filled with life that refreshes me. I often fail to comprehend Your majesty in such simplicity.

I give You thanks and call upon Your name.

Amen!

June 14

> "I can do all things through You who gives me strength."
> Philippians 4:13

Lord, it's only when I forget this that false fear invades, and it temporarily blinds me.

But then I remember again that You in me guides and greases the slide. I should not hide but abide in thee and watch those fears flee as it's no mystery that Your wings are upon me. When I face fear, I wake up from this temporary illusion as I return to my breath and listen to Your whisper again. I can do all things to overcome or achieve or just be. You, Lord, give me strength.

Thank You, Father.

Amen.

_____
_____
_____
_____
_____
_____
_____
_____
_____
_____
_____

June: Gratitude

June 15

God and Lord, You are the endless provider and giver, never ceasing. It is I, the receiver, who seemingly is so often unable to simply BE and receive!

So today, I simply, with an open heart, stand upon the land You provided and the sky You breathed into existence and lift my hands with my palms open to Heaven to fully receive Your blessing, mercy, and grace. The sun of Your creation warms my face, and my red cheeks are now the fuel warming my soul.

You are the father of all, which means You are My Father.

Above all earthly fathers, Happy Father's Day to thee. You are the Father in Heaven who keeps all promises, knows no distance, and is the creator of love, for You are love.

May I live a life of love as it honors You, my perfect Father in Heaven!

Amen!

_____
_____
_____
_____
_____
_____
_____
_____
_____
_____

June 16

More than knowing ABOUT You, I know You, my gracious Lord and God. When I meditate on the hope and truth I AM and HAVE in You, it causes me to believe, know, and feel You. I know I never really die; in the end, I transcend closer to You. Your energy is in me; that's where purity and clarity reside. This creates peace that receives Your expression in me and all things. I smile, and my eyes are quiet as I see the way. I am of the Heavenly realm and am only temporarily in this world physically, but Your peace is everlasting and an unbreakable lease calling me to live permanently beyond. I know how lame shame is, so I shed that which led me to falsity. I now practice the blessing of Your grace that shines upon my face.

When I am sad, it can progress to mad, but then I remember as a lad, I could see eternity when my mind was open. I will be in eternity, as the evidence is in my dreams.

Amen!

June 17

I call upon You. I call on the name of my Lord, who I adore! I awake and say, "Hey, not sure where this day will take me, but I am secure whichever way." You are my security and truth. You allow me to exist in perpetuity, for my voice commands my place as Yours for all that's in store.

In this, I'm alert and confident as I move, for it's You, my Lord. I trust as I must and know everything that's in store is Your choreography.

As I pursue the winding road from here to there, I do so with the confidence that serenity is before me. My ultimate story is surrounded in Your glory, which was, is, and always will be.

Amen!

June 18

Lord of Love, Lord of Life, the Lord of the core of my soul. I fully delight in You. I accept Your unconditional love, mercy, and grace. I claim it as the cornerstone of my life on earth and in Heaven. It's my full recognition that as I rest in and blindly trust in You, all illusions of pain, loneliness, and separation transform now and forevermore into security, serenity, harmony, and unity of purpose.

In this, I rest . . . in this I trust . . . as it's my rightful inheritance as a child of God.

Amen!

June: Gratitude

June 19

Lord God, may my deepest gratitude be present in my heart for all You do, provide, and guide. Lord, may I surrender my doubts and deepen my trust. God, all is well. I know wholeness, safety, harmony, and abundance, and it is unfolding naturally as You bless me.

As I loosen my grip on attachments, my arms become open for You. May my feeling of goodness grow within, for You are the source of unfolding goodness. I give thanks as I learn to rest in You. I deepen my trust in You and let go of all that causes me to resist, and I attach to the things holding me from my freedom in You.

The more I see the world, the less of your Heavenly wholeness I see. Open the eyes of my spirit, quiet the doubt, and allow the surrender I resist. I simply need to fully rest and trust deeply in You. When I resist, I am doubting Your very goodness. Lord, You know best. Have Your way in my soul today in a deeper and greater way than in the days past. Lord, fix my eyes upon You! For You are the true love, who gave me the breath of life!

With my deepest love, Lord. Amen!

_____
_____
_____
_____
_____
_____
_____

June 20

Lord my God, designer of my soul, architect of my eternal spirit, free me and fill me with Your energetic flow. Rid me of all worldly deceptions that keep me from being the intensity of complete delight that You designed my existence for. These Heavenly truths are the pure delight of Your design. You make me perfect, for I am what You alone designed. That's more than all right; that's a call out for an alleluia to You, MY GOD! Hit the Delete button on my inner workings that create the lies of separation, scarcity, and isolation. The ego of comparison and the deceit of superiority and inferiority distract me from You. But in total equality, You created my spirit for freedom. When I am in harmony with all Your children, You delight in me.

Lord, may You delight in me today, for that alone will be the ultimate joy this heart could ever know! I love You, Daddy in Heaven! I am Your Child!

June: Gratitude

June 21

Lord my God, allow me to live today fully awake. May I be purposeful, not mechanical. Give me sensitivity for the hurting, encouragement for the struggling, and gladness with the joyful. Allow me to live in harmony with all I meet and influence.

Train my mind to naturally give gratitude, grace, and mercy.

When we are living more of this day in gratitude, I have less time to worry, so may I be grateful for everything and everybody who surrounds me. Make me an instrument of inspiration, and may the words of my mouth flow from Your river of grace.

Lord, instill in me an unspeakable joy that says to all I know that the love they see in me comes from You. You wait on Your throne of grace, mercy, and endless Love!

I ask in You! Amen!

June 22

God, You have placed me here for such a time as this. You reveal my precise purpose today. I give thanks, have gratitude, and receive Your protection. I know it requires darkness in the ground for a seed to grow into a plant. With this in mind, I wait for consciousness to come from misery shed.

May I be free from misery and have peace from Heaven to know, feel, and share holy hope.

I search for Your face. May it renew my spirit to be Your servant of love. As I carry Your Holy Spirit at the center of my being, let the places I go become brighter as the encouragement and love of Your presence are felt by those around me. When I know Your truth as a certainty, I transcend the world's constructs, and I become a reflection of Your own presence.

Today, may I see You when I meet someone new and carry Your compassion to them. God of love, allow me today to receive fully so I may give grace freely, forgive myself and others, and create a calm in the storm of the day. Might I surrender cleverness in self for total trust in You. I will exit the stage of worldly performance and embrace Heavenly humility.

Thank You for this new day that I can greet and accept as the gift You designed for me to unwrap and experience.

For You are God, and I am Yours!

Amen!

_____
_____
_____

June 23

Lord, You are the reason I have hope. Your breath gave me life. Your love creates my energy. You are the source of all I have. You give me hope even in my grief and temper my ego in my success. Your greatness extends beyond any conceived earthly glory of man, for Heavenly glory is only for You, God. Your glory ignites all the good I can do with a glad heart, grateful for Your favor and the lessons that enrich my soul.

I delight in You. My spirit dances upon Your earth and awaits the unspeakable joy of being in its rightful place in Heaven, where my spirit will return just as You planned. Until then, I'll just learn and practice my dance and sing here.

Amen!

June 24

God, thank You for my life. Thank You for everyone I have known as family, friend, and even foe. For ALL is by Your design to bring me closer to You. First by comfort and then by growth. What do I gain if I only love those You have given to love me?

Even those You've given me I have at times disappointed, taken for granted, or couldn't see in the haze of my own ego. Often those who have offended me, minimized, or hurt me, gained more attention in my mind.

Help me to see that both my shortcomings and my challenges were to awaken my soul and grow my dependence for grace, forgiveness, and mercy, leading to greater peace in You.

Every moment of every day that I was surrounded by those I love filled me with purpose, and the lonely days of grief were both to bring me to Your protective arms and to be comforted by Your joy-giving embrace.

My life, love, family, critics, and business are all in and by You, Lord. May I receive it all for Godly unity with the family of humanity that You have created. It's awesome to be Your created.

With Gratitude to my God!

June 25

I give You gratitude, Lord.

Even when my heart is far from that instinct. My circumstances may be a struggle, but I give You gratitude, for You are the hope that pulls me through. I give You gratitude. I feel it in my soul, and before it becomes an action, I give You gratitude. This is what awakens me as You allow me to see the finish line of me in Your arms. I give You gratitude.

The journey is often lonely, sad, and in sorrow. I cannot always see the lessons, but You are transforming my trust to deepen my dependence upon You, so in the end, I give You gratitude. There will be days that I can see more clearly. I feel You nearly, and I see in the end, You had a purpose through it all to allow me to learn grace. I receive forgiveness, the price that allows me to open my heart, receive Your love, and end it all to walk Your streets in perpetual joy eternally.

I give You, my God, total and complete gratitude.

Amen!

_____
_____
_____
_____
_____
_____
_____
_____

June 26

You, God, are not distant as You are within my very own being.

You, God, restore me from sorrow to joy.

You, God, do not bring fearful judgment as You are restoring forgiveness and grace.

You, God, are not the tyrant and creator of fear; You are the definition of Love, who washes fear away and makes me pure.

The inventions of the deceitful stories of man, who create distance from me and You, is utter trash.

You created hope, healing, and contagious joy in me, and You bring light from darkness and life from death. Fully trusting in You makes me walk nearer to be home with You. I am a bearer to Your truth in me and me in You!

You, God, provided and made me; therefore, I have enough, and I am enough just as You created me.

With You, I have enduring eternal peace.

Amen!

June: Gratitude

June 27

I AM no longer, but I never was, for it's You in ME who is, was, and will be.

My freedom is from learning that as I heard this truth and read it in Your word, memorizing, reciting it, and even repeating and sharing it, it did not set me free to delight in fully experiencing You. Now that I have discovered BEING IT, Your promises and words become a transforming of the spirit. I now can sit in Your presence, Lord, and receive You.

The life of one I cherished had to be with You in Heaven. Before I could hear the whisper of someone I trusted and loved on earth, I had to recognize it was Your voice in Him, speaking to me.

Thank You, for Your love really does endure forever. Those are not just words but Your reality!

Amen!

June 28

Lord, give me the gratitude that frees me to generosity.

Every good thing comes from You. May it then come through me to those I know, love, and meet. Make me a gift from You with a spirit of generosity. All is from You, so may I not withhold any good You desire to do through me.

Give me the trust that allows me to give without fear of my personal needs. This practice brings me joy.

Through such charity, we become wealthy, and if we are stingy, we lose everything.

Give me the freedom and trust to be a cheerful giver.

Amen!

June 29

My strength is in the Lord. My loving care is His Spirit, and the Father is my protection. There is no position that I am in that is a surprise to Him as He has every step that I walk accounted for. I lean in and fully trust Him, and when I fall to concern or fear, I remember He is always near.

Instead of fear when I can hardly bear the challenges I face, I thank Him for keeping me from all disgrace.

I walk with this gratitude in mind so I will never be spiritually blind.

Amen!

June 30

Your steadfast love is new every morning. This renews my hope daily. When I seek discovery in Your purpose in each circumstance that unfolds, I am lifted up. You renew me, restore relationships, instill compassion, and bring unity in my community. May I be forgiven and quick to forgive. May I believe the best intent in others and my intention be of kindness.

Take from me anything that prevents harmony. Use me for Your purposes of goodness, kindness, and compassion.

Thank You, Lord, for walking beside me every day.

Amen.

JULY: UNITY

July: Unity

July 1

Help me, Lord, and forgive me. Take away the aggression that keeps me from you. Increase my ability to be self-aware so that I am fair in my interactions with others.

I want to be free of this obsession with constantly analyzing everyone around me. Judging and comparing only distorts my view of myself and others. I have no control over my neighbors, but your gift of free will allows me to improve myself.

When met with this thought, may I focus on my own growth and let others be.

We are all different yet made equally in your image. May that be enough for me to surrender to the unity only you can provide.

I see that everyone is free to be just as you created. When I see a tree, I don't judge based on its size or color! I just see the beauty you created it to be.

So, may this become natural for me to greet humanity with the expectation of beauty in your creation.

Amen.

_____
_____
_____
_____
_____
_____
_____
_____

July 2

I am as God created me. I am His, eternally His. This is what makes me whole and free without placing me higher on the tree in any hierarchy. From a distance, the leaves on a tree are not known for individuality. But it's how they advance the whole crowd without being boastful or proud. One leaf doesn't shade the ground, but together, they provide peace and serenity. I'm unique, but together we are all complete.

Amen.

July: Unity

July 3

Give me an increasing desire every hour to strive for peace. Give me the ability to see You within me and in everyone else I know and see.

How easy it will be to give the benefit of the doubt if I see You all about. Grace naturally flows, and unity is contagious in our community.

This magic will ignite a slow burn, dissolving the confusion and worldly chaos caused by separation. I will always believe the best as I see with Heaven's bright light and its holy might. As I look into others' eyes, I find the beauty of YOU!

Amen

_____
_____
_____
_____
_____
_____
_____
_____
_____
_____
_____
_____
_____
_____

July 4

Grant me patience, humility, and compassion to fuel a spirit of unity. This is the reality You meant for me.

When I'm in a hurry, my heart's eyes are blocked by pride. Completely blind, I hide my kindness inside.

So, open me up to patience and humility, creating equality for all. Your spirit encourages me to love others, which in turn shows love for You. I ask that this Heavenly reality generates compassion that leads to an incredible unity in my entire community. In this, I hear my Father's voice and rejoice!

Amen.

July 5

Your healing invites me not just to lay my wounds aside but for me to surrender my burdens, doubt, and worry to You. At the end of my journey, I will finally be able to see all the ways You work to make me perfect like You. Everything that made no worldly sense had my highest purpose in mind in Your perfect plan. Shaped by Your beauty, I walk a path forged to reflect You.

All those things that falsely divided me from my brothers are Your ultimate tools to build a magnificent unity. I sought significance through illusions that only divided me from everyone, even my friends. You designed my role on this earth specifically for me. I will shine Your light through me, creating a holy unity with those around me.

I could ask for nothing more!

Amen.

July 6

I am one with You. I am one with love. As the wave cannot separate itself from Your ocean, I can never be separated from You. I am a wave of Your ocean.

There is only WE in our reality, and I ask that any lesser thought flees.

I am fortified, satisfied, and have gratitude for my answered prayers.

May I understand the beauty within heartache and accept the heartache within beauty.

You infused my story with serenity that enables me to see You in me and in everyone I meet. My truest purpose is to represent You who sent me.

Amen.

July: Unity

July 7

I willingly invite Your joy into my heart as I share it with those around me. May I not judge or compare myself with others. Your call to me is unique and special—just for me—as your call to others is individually unique for them.

When I can't understand the challenges I face, I remember You even have a count on the hairs of my head.

We will continue to love You here on earth as we will forever in Heaven.

Amen.

July 8

I have been justified and reconciled, and God has made peace with me through His righteous cleansing. All things are renewed, restored, and reconciled.

This assurance of hope in Him makes me free. He fills my cup, no matter how difficult, challenging, or complicated. My final chapter has already been written, ending in bliss. What I face in this life cannot minimize the glory, which, in the end, is magnified by the agony I overcome. Any pain is temporary as I'm Heaven bound, waiting for unity with all the children of God.

May we become an earthly outpour of peace, compassion, understanding, and love. I want no thought in my mind other than the hope for the freedom of all tribes and nations. His grace includes all things and all people in Heaven and on earth. We are all His!

My story is not a mystery or even a dark comedy, as its hero anticipated every failure and raised me up beyond all understanding.

Often, I get lost in the day, out of control emotions, causing me to forget. But then I look up beyond the human haze and gain Heavenly clarity. For the author of this story is the creator of my being.

Amen!

_____

_____

_____

_____

July 9

Lord, my gracious, forgiving, and unconditionally loving God. You reset my heart every day. When I get lost in this world of man-made mountains, You give me a glimpse of the magnificence of Your entire creation. Each leaf on Your trees waves to me, reminding me of Your love like the magnificent dove flying above.

Then I see there is no hierarchy, for we are all beautiful souls learning to love just like You from above. Seeing through each other's eyes, I realize we are all in the process of becoming just like Jesus. Each of us is part of Your thumbprint, my creator, sustainer, king, and glorious friend. You are the source of love that is meant to be my friend. We are Yours with unique stories and are all equal in the end!

Amen.

July 10

The awakening and grounding of my life is the peacefulness of my soul. My human existence is no longer a stage show, nor do I have to create some great feat. I am now ready to meet both the elite and the struggling, for we are all family. I can let go of my mental distortions and be just as God gifted me to be.

Life is to be lived and received by everyone, including me. It is not a race, a beauty contest, or a wrestling match. It's to be welcomed as a great huddle of humanity whose happiness is guaranteed if only we can see and receive its simplicity. God gave me this gift, and it is only a struggle when I choose trouble when I can instead be in a Heavenly bubble.

The moment my heart pursues the simple act of being kind, I am no longer blind to the beauty of the world. I am satisfied, and nothing but light takes me higher than a kite, getting me through every night right back to His might.

Amen.

July 11

Thank You, God, for this day that I greet. I meet it with the assurance that it's a gift from You. I know that each person I meet or just pass by is by Your design. Each soul that surrounds me was created by You for Your pleasure, just as I was.

When I see each of them as a piece of You, it creates an equal ground to commune and see with love, rebuking judgment. Compassion, understanding, and empathy for others grant me an internal peace that astounds me.

As I draw nearer to You, my assumptions and worldly ways that drew me into comparison and separation dissolve into understanding, unity, and community. Lord, I now feel the euphoria of love for which You placed the beat of my heart within me.

I delight in You, Your creation, and Your created.

May the trauma of man's creation submit itself to the delight of Heaven's promises.

Remind me of the delight of the unity that my soul thirsts for. Destroy the man of the world within me who dances on the worldly stage of approval.

I am who You say I am, resting comfortably in the soul that You unleashed on this earth to encourage and love others. I now realize Your full presence on Earth as it is in Heaven.

Amen!

_____
_____
_____
_____

July 12

My merciful God, allow me to comprehend that when I stop struggling, I have freedom; when I have freedom, I stop struggling, and then there is nothing but Joy.

This is Your circle of life for me, which all my collective experiences prepared me for. A faith in You, held tight by my trust, releases me into a circle of faith and a cycle of life that lights my soul and illuminates the path for others.

May these truths allow me to serve up friendship with an overflowing serving spoon and to lay down and destroy the knife of separation.

God created me to be in harmony with His people. May I know and share You, not because of anything in me but simply because it's who You made me to be . . . just like You!

Amen.

July 13

How callous can my heart become? When I separate my heart of love from my mind that thirsts for approval of man, I become less of who You made me to be. Lord, may I have the strength of my authenticity and the softness of heart for others who speak loudest within me. The approval and applause of man distorts my spirit's nature.

When I am weak in spirit, my mind is driven with concern of disapproval and rejection of man. What is the cost when my earthly presence seeks acceptance, approval, and worldly accolades of wealth and companionship of callous men?

My joy in You! That's what is at stake!

I think I'll live for eternity rather than for the finality of my earthly existence. Remind me, Lord, when the decisions unfold in life.

May I trust You and desire to please You and take joy in who You created me to be and who to bless.

I forget, Lord, that You knew everything all along, and all my struggle melts to bliss in Your arms.

The story ends HEAVENLY!

Amen!

July 14

Lord, help me to see harmony when my heart pursues confrontation.

If I truly love You first, the energy of my spirit compels me to love my neighbor as myself.

Why do I look for differences and judgments and yearn for superiority.? You who is in Me calls me to greater harmony, unity, and peace. May I desire first to lift others up. Then, I, too, rise to the heights of the eternal promise of Heaven's peace.

May You calm my physical being when it's stirred by separation, creating this pain of isolation. Allow me to be a call to love at those times when my human instinct is to draw differences. Then, I will become the peacemaker You created me to be.

I am not waiting until Heaven but have a foretaste of Your Heavenly spirit on earth.

Amen!

July 15

When I compromise the truth and value, baiting hostilities, pitting people against each other becomes prized, monetized, and honored. Then, it is I who creates the existence of hell on earth!

The lies of the devil replace the love in my eternal spirit. Then, I am deceived into thinking I have won an earthly battle when I have only saddened the spirit of God.

The battle is Yours, and I am Your warrior, not my own earthly general. What does it gain if You gain the whole world but compromise Your soul and if the breath of God in Your lungs is replaced by a rallying cry of hate, division, and judgment?

I surrender my soul to live the love of the Lord. I will no longer worry about winning, collecting, and knowing. Instead, may I delight in God's good and gracious gifts of friendship, companionship, encouragement, and love.

May I consume myself with how I can bless, encourage, and love rather than conquer, collect, and divide.

Might my full and joyous delight be in You Lord, and might I see You in the one before me.

Amen!

July 16

May I love kindness, and may I deeply desire to be in unity with my neighbor.

Grant me the humility that allows me to learn from those the world sees as disadvantaged. Give me compassion and understanding for those who walk a different path, think differently, and are not just like me. I wish to see they are just as You have made them to be.

My tribe should not limit my love to those who have commonality with me. May I see Your grace, love, and mercy in growing abundance as I give and receive Your love to all those You have given me to know, meet, or even pass on the street. May I grow and respect that You have a unique and perfectly loving rapport with each of Your children, not needing my interpretation, judgment, or correction. You love us each uniquely and perfectly, in which I can do nothing but mimic Your love. As I reveal more of You in me, it's my way to be a doer of the faith You have given me that sets my spirit free! May my light of You in me be contagious.

Amen!

July 17

Lord, use me to bring unity where there is division and peace where there is acrimony.

Allow me to act from my core of Your unconditional love for me.

Might that total trust part the clouds that prevent me from clearly seeing who You are in me in my conversations of passion.

May the dark clouds of this world give way to Your love and peace.

May I no longer place my own wounds, hurts, and disappointments before who I am in You. They separate me from the energy of Your love to whom You give me to know, influence, and be Your goodness to.

I want to care more about Your compassion alive in me than any other thing that distorts Your unconditional love for all of Your people.

Thank You, Lord, for giving us a heart after Your very own.

Might I be worthy by first being a purveyor of Your kindness and empathy.

Amen!

_____
_____
_____
_____
_____
_____

July 18

Thank You for the freedom You send me in the form of music. Your universal language makes my spirit speak, know, and understand You in me. The language that brings unity and defies separation is from You.

Ignorance that rejects Your inspiring song doubts Your magnificent creation of man's spirit. If we can openly see Your works, we can receive Your healings. May I never again miss the voice of God in song.

The harmony of my soul is one of Your greatest gifts to me. I need only open my ears to hear You from another who shares this gift within. Music allows us to break free from being trapped in our bodies and to sing, dance, and fly to the rhythm of our souls!

Thank You, Lord. I think I'll dance to "As the Saints Go Marching In" for eternity. I am in that number!

Yahoo! Amen!

July: Unity

July 19

God in Heaven, Lord of my life, create in me an energy of rest and healing. Unleash in me a peace that allows me to be an encouragement to others. Give me a heart of empathy for those hurting. May I speak words that uplift. May I have Your heart of love to share and guide. May I have the humility to hear Your words through others You have, by Your intention, placed with me today.

Might I feel Your call to unity and be inspired to be the one who desires to learn rather than teach.

Today, I wish to be filled by observing Your grace through others in my community.

May I be alert, receptive, and encouraged by Your children. We are Your people. We huddle together but stand alone. We are both independent for our strength in You but huddle together to serve others in Your name. From the huddle, I have the strength to stand for Your call to one another. We gather to be fueled by Your spirit through others. Lead me to the right huddle today.

May my heart be open and my ears attentive to simply receive Your word of grace.

Amen!

_____
_____
_____
_____
_____
_____
_____

July 20

Lord, give me the resolve to simply do what is right. Allow me to be unselfish. Grant me the ability to give the free grace and forgiveness You have already given me.

No meaningful pardon comes from the powers of man, but the true freedom is the one You have granted me.

May this trust in Your truth free me and deaden my ego and give full life to my spirit within.

Approval from man and the endless torment of negative thoughts cease when my trust is truly in You. So often, I hold on as this is left to my control. Freedom begins and sustains in You alone. May You overcome all in me that keeps me from eternal bliss in You in the here and now.

And while I'm here, may I be a purveyor of Your love, kindness, and forgiveness abundantly and freely!

Amen, so be it now and forevermore!

July: Unity

July 21

Free me of the comparison and judgment that distorts my Godly vision. May I see You in the person before me, and might it reflect who You are in me, bringing a perfect unity of Your created.

The dawn of a new day brings renewed refreshment of who I am as Yours.

They in me and You in me make a unity that delights, as I have discovered true spiritual beauty.

Not in wanting, waiting, or wishing but in being and experiencing the power of now.

This moment is for receiving and being the blessings in the moment for which You designed and created me to know, delight, and be in freely and without distraction.

So be it! I receive it!

Amen!

July 22

Give me strength of heart, Lord, to face the day.
    Inspire the step of my foot to walk with goodness.
    Allow the expansion of my presence to be welcoming.
    May the Spirit be fully present with whoever You give me to be with today.
    May the distractions that divide us give way to the mutual reality of Your breath in each of us that provides a bridge to harmony.
    We are Yours, and You are OUR God. God of all and all creation . . . we count on You alone to rule and judge, and may we dedicate and devote ourselves to brotherly love.

July 23

Lord, Your love is lavish. Place in my hand the brush that paints the strokes of encouragement in the lives of others.

Give me the words to inspire Your good, the eyes to see Your spirit, and the dance in my step that brings joy to others.

Extinguish the paranoia that creates separation. Allow me to err on the side of trusting others, for You are in them, and You are protection. I fear no man because You alone are the author of my story.

I start, endure, and end by Your touch! I feel You within. I grow daily in confidence and certainty as every moment gains greater clarity of who You are in me and who I am in You!

Amen!

July 24

Lord, You have said You prepared in advance the good works I would do. May I freely allow it to unfold in this world. May I not inhibit Your love through me by fear of man or grandiosity of self.

Give me the courage to speak the truth kindly with love. May I know it's You who has chosen to use me for Your good, surrendered to You.

Keep me from the fear of judgment of man so I can do the good You planned. May I not seek credit or glory on earth but desire it in Heaven with You.

Minimize in me the delight of the things of this world that create illusions, such as proximity to power or believing that provision comes from any other than You. Abundance is by Your grace, and may I use it to glorify You and serve my brother.

To the extent it's up to me, may I grow to desire unity and peace that leads to You. May Your love live and grow in me!

Amen!

July: Unity

July 25

Lord, heal the poison in the nervous system of our nation.

Open the good heart of America that You graced this world with.

Might we again be the hope of the light of our Lord that fueled our forefathers' dreams.

Where people would delight in unity and the common good. Where we championed brotherly love, washing away our petty grievances with one another. Where we were certain that Kindness will bring the compassion that erases ignorance. Where the common good was known by peace, purity, and the pursuit of goodness.

Lord, take the anger from the core of mankind away. Might we be stopped in our tracks and awaken and see You in each other that compels us to see Your light of love within the one before us. May we comprehend our ignorance, giving us the root of forgiveness. Where comparison ceases, compassion begins.

Melt the hate created by illusions of ghosts who never existed, creating resentment, anxiousness, and poison from illusions of people we never met. We were told stories for the purpose to divide, create resentment, and settle scores that are the illusions of the mind.

Bring us together, united by a higher purpose. Love from You that unites all of us is the underpinning of the United States of America!

Amen!

_____
_____
_____

July 26

God in Heaven, creator of Earth and all creation, You are my peace, protection, and purpose. Any worldly problem is my illusion, as there is nothing that can happen that has not been purposeful, useful, and by Your will. Your provision fills my every need.

You fill me with purpose and healing. You call me to Yourself to awaken my soul. Erase all doubt and allow me to see that every challenge is for me to trust You and know You more. You lead me, inspire me, and provide me gifts. You've surrounded me with the people You gave me to be Your love to, and I receive Your living love on earth through them.

May we live in harmony and desire peace. May this be our desire over creating the lie that we are in control. Prevent the deceptions of the mind to surrender to the spirit breathed into me by Your breath. May separation give way to harmony, creating a unity among all Your people.

Amen!

July 27

Grant me wisdom and compassion, gracious God.

May the Heavens reign down empathy, compassion, and understanding to my heart to share with all I meet.

May I see Your face in every face I pass so as to constantly be reminded of You in others.

May my deepest desire be in unity by eliminating the concept of hierarchy and replacing it with equality, understanding, and care.

Allow me to grow my potential for compassion, restoration, and peace.

May Your filling of grace abound in my spirit and bless others.

May I grow in Your goodness to delight in doing good and feeling Your love through loving Your created and Your creation.

Amen!

July 28

You, Lord, are kind to the evil and the ungrateful. I struggle to love my enemies and forgive those who hurt me.

Destroy what keeps me from freely being Your grace, mercy, and loving kindness. May Your realities of renewal draw and create within me a pull toward Your aura of love, light, and renewal.

As the roots of a tree freely nourish its neighboring roots, might I be free to feel that same natural act of unity.

May my energy-driven dreams dissolve the fear of my illusions.

Might I be as Your natural creation and have no knowledge of separation but simply know the harmony of Your design of creation.

Amen!

July 29

The soul of man is neither black or white, Chinese or American, rich or poor, Christian or Jew.

It's simply God's creation within.

It's not any of these, yet it is all of these. It's all of mankind and all of creation. It's all for one and one for all. If not understood here, it will have clarity and comprehension beyond. It's all uniquely designed for the magnification of the Glory of God. He inspires us to an individual journey to be His call of man. It's the fate of grace as I rest and trust in Him.

I am in the hands of God and the comfort of the palms of His grace.

Amen!

July 30

Lord my God, may I understand humility as You describe and prescribe for me.

It's not a tool to minimize but a method to maximize You in me by leveling all with me and me with them. These are my brothers and sisters, and I am theirs. You, as our Father, delight uniquely and differently in each of us.

When I humbly stand next to them and, through humility, accept their help to strengthen me, I am closer to thee. It's when I think I have to earn my way and overcome others to stand closer to You that You seem farther. I'm closest to You when I love the others. You created for me to know and to know me by the opening of my heart to all I see.

You created the truth for me, so I now comprehend that humility comes before honor. This is done in creating connection, not separation. May I awake when a false sense of superiority appears. I so often do what I do not desire. Humility is a motivation to glorify You, my God, instead of a motivation to ignore my own accomplishments after all. You gave it all to me. This glorifies and magnifies You in me, which is the way I want to be.

So be it.

Amen!

_____
_____
_____
_____
_____
_____

July 31

Revenge, score-settling, conquering, and determining fairness are all pursuits that I chase when I'm not truly trusting You.

You alone determine the call and purpose of my being and soul. It's when I take on any of these roles that belong to You alone that I am denied the permanent pleasure of peace that I have increasingly come to know.

When I conquer another, it's Your other equal child who receives the loss for which I cause You to mourn.

May my heart be quelled of resentment so as to cease the idea of revenge at its spark.

Father, creator, sustainer, and equalizer, give me a pure heart with intentions that live in the truth and trust of Your eternal promises. This is when all scores are settled with this Godly judgment, and only Your peace is to behold. This will be when the Heavenly dance delights the streets of gold.

In this world, I can become so lost in keeping score, appearances, and tallying rights and wrongs. I forget to see the unity within the image of You in the human before me that I failed to see. For as I look really closely at the one I scorned and as I gaze into their eyes, I stop in amazement. MY Lord, forgive me, for NOW, I see it's You in those eyes meant only to reach, teach, and awaken me. Now I'm new and in harmony with You and the spirit within me.

Amen!

_____
_____
_____
_____

AUGUST: PEACE

August: Peace

August 1

I cast my anxiety on You. You allow me to see, know, and grow in each thought that passes through me. Make me Your compassion and my experience of grace.

I confess my blindness to the injustices of the world. In You, I see with clarity. I see Heavenly, restorative justice for all on the horizon in Your divine love. Your word promises me this inheritance and cannot be spoiled and is kept for me. You are eternal, and You are love—love that Your spirit planted in my heart.

May You be glorified in my love. For Your promises are written on my heart.

Amen.

August 2

Fear and doubt can only threaten me when I allow them to satiate me.

Letting them overwhelm is only a state of mind that I choose to not let control me.

When I see my God is full of grace, I no longer can have the space to contemplate the false projections of the horrors of this place.

Instead, I've found when I choose to ground myself in thanksgiving, fear and doubt are no longer about.

These things dissolve the moment I'm reminded God has a perfect plan for me. So I can turn that to glee and be free of that mental fear that I could hardly bare.

Everything I see is God's glory through all of my mind's chatter. For that clatter ceases with everything that truly matters. I will never embrace my sanity until I release my vanity. It's better to be part of the community than creating a hierarchy full of malarkey.

Amen.

August: Peace

August 3

May You lift negativity with grace and ease within me. Your promises create an optimism that balances my mind and opens my heart when I surrender to You. It's Your grace alone that brings me serenity, so Lord, remind me when I'm distressed that You are in each moment of challenge, calling me to surrender and trust. May I call on You daily. When I inhale Your love, I then exhale fear. Forgive me and free me when this does not come easy.

May all barriers of mental hijacking be replaced with Your light of grace.

May deep healing wash away the pain of the traumatic past so grace replaces my human craving for control. May I be a healing of positive energy, surrendering those things that keep me from being the closest reflection of Your light.

Amen!

August 4

I am a child of God. No reason to fear. You reign forever. You are the perfect Father.

As I gain greater glimpses of Your goodness, my concept of fear fades.

When I was so confused, I thought this world was about avoiding hell in the end, but You revealed to me my eternity begins with Heaven.

With this certainty, my life has no doubt now that I know what it's really about.

I am and will always be a child of God—what greater reason to rest in this truth!

So my motto is FFF: forget false fear.

Amen.

August 5

You have cautioned that if I am not made of love, I am nothing.

I'm certain I am something, so I understand I am love and was always meant to be. For you are my creator and love generator. When I fail to see from the eyes of my heart, my love is replaced with fear.

The fear that chases me dissolves when my heart hears your call. This is your warning and awakening to me: to be open and alive. I replace fear with your love and trust in your grace. Now, I see love in me. Your faith instills a gospel of love that keeps me full of hope and never at the end of my rope.

When I am asleep in spirit, I am temporarily deceived, only relieved by your power. I stand on the land you gave to me, surrendered fully in trust.

Amen!

August 6

I am the most in You when I think the least. To not have to know is everything.

My prayer is silent and unceasing. I cannot diminish or add to the unfolding of the day.

Let me let go of worry or what could have been as I learn to surrender to the state of love within.

May I accept and receive simply as things are, with no desire to control or change the events that are untold. My mind tells me to go where Heaven's river flows. May I be certain that the flow of Your energy places me where my transformation to be who You're calling me to be is my ultimate productivity.

I choose to give voice to this experience of faith's inner peace and unfold confidently in trust!

Amen.

August 7

Give me the wisdom to be free from worry and doubt. Fear has no value here because Your love gives me peace from above like a dove. It's these thoughts that free me of anxiety.

These passing emotions are my mind's dark invention, and once I'm aware, I no longer care about their danger. Your light of love breaks through any power they hold over me.

I am in Your loving presence, which makes me hopeful, complete, and secure.

Amen.

August 8

Help me, Lord, to see, feel, and know that we are all made in Your image. At the core, we are all woven from the same fabric of Your love. That is much more than I had in store on my own ability. May this change my eyes of judgment that have caused separation. With this growth before me, I am capable of seeing Your intended unity.

This promised freedom allows my heart to grow as I acknowledge that You are walking by my side. May I hear Your whispers of peace when I need You most. You ease the troubles of my heart with Your promise of serenity.

Amen!

August: Peace

August 9

May my anger become eclipsed by Your love. Holy Spirit, quiet the chaos of my ego. The peace within my soul has transformed my body, healing every anxious thought. I hope this peace can be seen in and through me, spreading its power to those around me. May the renewing of my mind create a calm beyond any I've known.

I know that what I ask is achieved by trusting Your perfection, which lifts everyone around me. Grow my trust. Then, my false doubt is dissolved in love. Your magnificence unveils the goodness of my life, founded in my trust of You.

Amen.

August 10

As I face the unfolding challenges, I am reminded that just as the storm rages above the sea, true reality lies in the calm depths beneath.

I am a struggling eagle learning to soar.

The highest relief from my struggles is in fully embracing Your peace without resistance. Lord, allow me to freely be this reality.

Amen.

August 11

I refuse to be drawn in by the drama and scandal of the world and instead focus on the peace in my soul.

I'm the expression of Your love and light, which frees me of anxiety. I release my repressed energy in favor of Your stillness.

My only reality is Your loving presence, and that is my ease and grace.

Thy will be done.

Amen.

August 12

The spirit of truth dwells with me and in me, which gives me strength and comfort in all I do. The peace of the walk in every step guides my talk, so I never balk. It is nourishment of milk to my bones, which sustains my strength in my core and assures I'm never a bore. I'm flowing with life from knowing this love You gave to me, the love and peace as brought from the most adorable dove straight from Heaven above. In all challenges and passing emotions, the eternal comfort of Your promise to me lasts through any temporary blast.

Any human attempt to attack me dissolves, as no judgment of man can cease this inner peace and internally grants Heavenly ecstasy.

Amen!

August 13

Lord, I surrender the complexities of humanity to You. May I worry about nothing and pray about everything.

The worry in my mind is not from trusting You, so knowing this, I cease and release that which is lesser than who You called me to be. With this in mind, my heart grows ten times, and I lose that overly worked mind as I no longer let it cruise, creating a mental bruise. I now can observe and create the perspective that it is You as my source to right my course.

When I simply rest in You, there is no anxiety. The calm surrounds and Your love abounds. It is all in me to feel my inner heal because You alone are the real deal. Now, I feel the comfort of Your spirit surrounding me, creating serenity.

Amen!

August 14

My attitude creates my altitude. My aptitude won't limit me, for You create the Godly attitude that exudes from me.

A life without struggle creates no muscle. I cannot hate but instead live in hope. I will forgive rather than be weighed down by grievance. I lost some time forgetting just who You made me to be. Now I can express the success in overcoming trials, for I'm riding a Heavenly crest. Your joy is my strength. Now my burdens are waiting, blessings soon to blossom, showing me what brings a perpetual glow.

I don't control what spins around me, but what my soul feeds on creates Your very own light in me. I don't hold onto misery as the energy that flows in me negates the lows, creating true joy in this old boy. All that might disappoint takes flight in the face of Your delight. All I am is what You will me to do and be . . . in inevitable eternity.

Amen!

August 15

My soul is Your presence of love within me. It is always there to calm troubled waters. I need only to remember it can never be lost.

The permanent and perpetual courage of the spirit's never-ending light kills my ignorance and fear. The light guides me on the creator's path, filling me with confidence as I journey through life on my way to eternity. As long as I follow You, there is no darkness.

My fear masquerades as a constant reality when the truth tells me that peace always anchors me. I just often need to be reminded that tranquility grounds the core of my spirit. The negative energy can be disturbing in this life, but it all dissolves in my human death, which gives way to the light that was always meant to be. The spirit is the cathedral that protects and leads me to the still pastures of peace.

Amen!

August 16

I take my solace in Your promises of peace in the age to come. I endure hardship while trusting who You are and with the full knowledge that You reign over all. You alone settle the disputes of mankind.

I will be filled with the knowledge of the Lord just as the water covers the sea. You will never abandon me; instead, allowing me glimpses of the world to come so that I may endure the difficult and take gratitude in the unfolding joy.

As I walk in the light of the Lord, who swallows up death forever, may I comprehend the mystery. You promise that one day, You will bring Your kingdom of peace, wiping away every tear, including my own. I will have a new heart and spirit as You have planned all along. I, a child of God, know that Heaven on earth will be everlasting, perfect harmony on earth just as it is in Heaven!

Amen!

August 17

God is love, so all is well. When my mind wanders into dark clouds, I repeat this one thought: God is love, so all is well.

I see it all from Heaven's call, this whisper that reminds me . . . God is love, so all is well.

This lifts me and returns me to my soul, who truly knows God is love, so all is well.

The peace is always here within, and all I need to do in a lonely hour is receive the renewing and remember His power. God is love, so all is well.

Amen.

August 18

Lord, make me a warrior of light, not a worrier. As a reflection of You, I love on earth the way I am loved by God. In this, I know no fear, only peace.

Lord, may my mind still long enough to recognize the bliss You have for me in the stillness. In honesty, I admittedly have run from the stillness that I speak of. It is easier to praise the tranquility of dwelling in Your presence, but it is often the last thing I do.

I conjured the thoughts of ferocious fear and aloneness. With the courage of this warrior's spirit, I can learn to come into stillness and wait. Here, I discover that what I feared is actually Your delight! For alone with You, I am in Your full presence. I stand before You to receive, be, and believe.

It is said You are before me, behind me, beside me, BUT I anxiously have filled all those places with self-importance, anxious ways, and mindless distractions.

But all of this has kept me from experiencing Your closest presence. I call to You to take fear from my grip and to rip me open to reveal Your light inside.

Amen!

August: Peace

August 19

Through the grace of my God, I see through the eyes of my Lord in stillness. This sounds idyllic, but as I approach it, I can fully rest and be near without fear. Create in me a peace that thirsts for Your presence and is prepared to receive all that I was created to be. This is who You delighted in creating, so I must stop berating. I could not add to this perfect batter, but try as I did; the fear and illusion only made my head get fatter.

When I realize Your peace is delightfully true, there is no real separation from You. For You are my eternal indwelling, the light within that silences all blight. It's only my body that's temporary and simply houses the perfection that extinguishes all damnation. On days of weakness, I deny who I am and instead claim myself as my own creation. The world's events and trauma distort the heart You created in me, only needing the correction to simply rest in You and just BE.

But how do I rest when anxiety rages, and depression surrounds me? Wow, I stop in my tracks as I remember You're one breath away. You are my calm within. The world I created is only an earthly illusion of control. But I must learn to trust You and rid myself of my human concerns. In the stillness, that peace is found, and You are always near.

Amen!

August 20

Lord, this is the time and place as I am living in a season of grace. At this pace, I find that my space and footing are no longer off-putting. I lift my hands to You and receive the renewal from the spool of Heaven, the pool that overflows and places this glow upon my face. I feel it and experience it from this place full of grace.

My heart is open, and my mind has been softened to receive the authenticity that frees me to know I am enough. I'm enlightened as all the blight is released from the depth of my fright. I am at ease, free from the freeze of confusion. But the light from Heaven's rays warms my soul and carries me everywhere I need to go.

God of love, God of light, renew my heart every night as this gives me Heavenly sight.

Amen

August: Peace

August 21

May the light of my soul extinguish the darkness that comes near me.

May fear never be truly near. The light within is bright as I open my heart right from the start of my day, receiving and believing the spirit whose call erases the fear of the fall. In the past, I rolled up into a ball, believing that terror threatened me, but as I awake, I have learned not to resist so the illusions don't persist. That misunderstanding created a false scare, but now I'm bare, open, and free as I was meant to be. My Holy Father has ordered my steps, and the stones whose water flowed torrentially in the end just made it smooth for me to walk across the sea.

In reality, I can just BE and believe, as insanity no longer takes hold of me. I'm free to be at home with all my brothers and sisters and receive the energy that is the source of my first earthly breath. I am renewed and refreshed!

Amen!

August 22

God of Heaven and ruler of my heart, overtake me in Your wholeness. Calm my spirit so it pours freely from You as a river flowing from Your grace.

God of Heaven, may the voice in my head be quieted by the Lord of my heart. So often, I find peace in You for it to give way to the worries and thoughts that speak through my controlling roommate, the voice in my head.

Renew me, give me a pure heart that's so rooted in Your absolute truths that I live from the God-centered heart You placed within me. May this be my ruling nature and the kingdom of my presence. May it bless those I meet. May this earthly presence of doubt be lessened as I fully receive a heart of love as Your gift to me.

Amen

August: Peace

August 23

The spaces of life are a taste of the eternal. It's that split second between shifting directions in Your breath that You find the greatest peace. If You focus upon this split second of time, it will grow as the time You live in the fullness of peace extends.

Quiet the mind and refocus the heart to awaken the fullness of the spirit. Let life unfold from the earthly to the Heavenly. This will open the gates of the soul, and life eternal is NOW and FOREVER!

In HIM, Amen, and Amen!

August 24

Lord, You have assured me that Your presence goes with me.

May this promise from You govern my reality and guide me with assurance and peace of Your promise.

Open the ears of my heart to clearly hear Your Holy Spirit.

May the peace that You have assured me grant me the peace that surpasses all understanding.

May it melt any block and overcome all difficulties to hear You, see You, and know You perfectly.

May the unity of faith bridge worldly disputes, transforming to union in spirit and truth within my soul.

So be it, as it is so.

Amen.

August 25

God of creation, God of my being, I receive with open arms the warmth of Your love. The knowledge of Your delight is the freedom my soul has in You. I surrender to You and allow all my fears to be replaced by total trust in You.

You are bigger than the world's perceived problems; may I rest in this truth. The pains of war in the world seem so far from Heaven's protection. Lord, may You bring comfort to our world. I can allow myself to be swallowed up in the chaos and division, but You are the God who brings order and unity. May my doubt melt and my trust become my one true anchor.

Help me see beyond the dictators of the world to look upon You alone. As I watch ego's war and nations attempt to devour others, may I see Your peace, protection, and purpose overcome and rule. You will restore peace and grant a new prosperity of provision. Free my mind's vision from misery, and deliver me into Your arms of unconditional love.

The empathy I have for the wounded and those fleeing their homes to safety pales in comparison to Your Godly compassion for every wounded and suffering soul.

Bring this world peace and end the hostility in the hearts of man. Temper the neurotic energy to renew the hope of who we are in You.

May I gain forgiveness where I have bitterness and resentment. May a deeper trust in You bring renewed optimism in our own hearts and land.

Amen!

_____
_____
_____

August 26

Dear God, I'm in no hurry—I have forever! Eternity knows no time, no deadline or urgency. The created anxiety of hurriedness only exists in the self-importance of man's ego. The constant confusion of my attempt to be my own creator creates temporary emptiness. But it's in being Your created that order and peace are found. Simply receiving Your order and love and perfection is where deep, everlasting peace waits for me.

Lord, the struggle was only in my mind, creating the illusion of separation through self-importance. This lie produces misery, separation, isolation, judgment, and comparison. This pecking order among my brothers and sisters created only distance from Your love. Through others that You have intentionally placed in my life, I can witness Your very own love until I am with You.

I now can see and willingly receive Your order, which brings unspeakable, enduring joy.

Amen!

August 27

Lord my God, how do I comfort the brokenhearted? Life has tragic realities. Oh God, where are You when life's wounds are unbearable? God, what can I do? What can I say at the moment hurt transpires beyond human understanding? How can I be Your earthly compassion to the devastation on earth? When those dearest are lost to those we know and love . . . how can we bring them to the entrance to the road of healing?

My empathy overwhelms my being, wishing I could change the clock when difficulty begins.

Only You are the real comfort in the deepest sadness.

God, have mercy on mankind. Give hope of Your light in the midst of darkness. May the hug of Your spirit be upon Your people in pain. May Your sustaining love be known. May Your tears from Heaven wash the stain of pain in hearts who feel separation. May knowing the unity of presence in You mend our soul. Lord God, use me in Your world to be Your comfort of love that gives Your grace earthly presence.

God, I pray for permanence of peace so all anxieties can be washed away. God, bring light to the darkness, as You have to know the darkness to see the light.

Amen!

August 28

Oh my God, allow my life on earth to be a foretaste of Heaven. Might my remaining days awaken my spirit fully and lead me to grow in love.

Use me to encourage and provide peace to each of Your children in my orbit.

Might my measure of purpose be the brightening light of hope inside me. May this be contagious to those in my path.

Help me see everyone in the context of Your miracles and intentions within my being and theirs.

Might I see You in them, freeing me of judgment of them and them of me.

Might I know that as I remain in Your flow and design, this is what makes my worldly work a joy to know.

Your designed plan unfolds on the gliding path of purpose en route to my eternal home.

Let Your assurance allow delight in me.

May this internal presence of peace be felt by others as You use me for the plans You had.

I will come to recognize and trust more deeply that Your design all along will unfold as Your eternal plan. You are the great architect of my life, breath, and reality for Your purposes and my joy.

You alone are the conductor, and I and all I have come to know are Your very own human orchestra of grace, mercy, and purpose.

I hold my palms open to simply receive!

Amen!

August 29

Your strong arms of love surround me. The peace of Your spirit is my encouragement. The presence of Your grace created my compassion. My journey is blessed when I let go and rest calmly in You. May the Wandering mind take rest to become my best embrace in the simplicity of Your peace. This is obtainable serenity.

Amen.

August 30

Dear God, place in me kindness that comes directly from You.

Lord, I know this is where peace comes from. Give it freely to me, and I will share it. It is You through me to others. Open my heart of humility to have a soft heart that receives as much as it desires to give peace.

Take from me all regret, and allow me to see peace as the building blocks of discovering Heavenly living.

Jonathan Lockwood has said to "forgive others, not because they deserve forgiveness, but because you deserve peace."

Lord, I desire to have Your peace and, in sharing it, become Your peacemaker.

Amen!

August 31

Nature's call is Your voice, my Lord. The beauty You extend is also within. The bird of the air's magnificence is equal to the vitality of the vision You have gifted to me.

The roots that ground a tree are as deep as its outward height, just as the depth of my spirit grounds my being.

The power of the flow of the river of life guides the direction of my path entrusted to You.

May my vision have spiritual clarity, my soul know peace, and my trust in You grow more confident daily.

Amen!

SEPTEMBER: CHILD OF GOD

September 1

The only identity for me personally and permanently is as Your child, my Lord and my God. This is the ultimate comfort, as You are the Creator, Sustainer, and Savior of my soul. All of the rest will one day fall from me as it's only a worldly game. I'm not an extension or projection of others but simply the one You made me to be. But why do I seek approval, affirmation, opinion, and assurance from others when this is only between my Father and me? I am enough because I'm exactly as You made me to be. May I receive at the deepest possible level the assurance and knowledge of Your love with never a doubt.

I say it with ease that You love me passionately, but I need to more deeply receive and believe. Strengthen my assurance as only You can in understanding Your unconditional love in this world of conditions, contritions, comparison, guilt, and shame as we're always looking for others to blame.

May in me Your unquestioned love reign.

Amen.

September 2

May I be filled with mercy as You are merciful. The more I can represent You, the more good I can do to be used by You. We complicate this world when our simple purpose is to love just like You. I've worked tirelessly to stand out from the crowd sometimes by being really loud, but the peace I seek is found in quiet unity with a friend in need. I'm now hearing Your whispers to allow me to intuitively be like thee.

I have found harmony in seeing how I am like You, creation like creator. As Yours, I was always bound to find my peace of mind in resting in You as I have now learned to do.

Amen.

September 3

I am what nature created me to be, in acceptance of what I was meant to be. That is my road to be happy. It's not a feeling or passing emotion but a flight into God's light. It needs no announcement but instead just acceptance, ending misery. When I resisted You, the crossroads of my ego made me think, "Just who is it they want me to be?"

As my ego was so busy creating this stage act, my soul was waiting to welcome me back. Fear is fueled by making a false me, but God reminds me of my identity. He is delighted with the rosebud, who is at peace and fully satisfied in its own bloom, no pride, only humility. My humanity confounded this example of simplicity. For when I'm simply me, as I was created to be, it's in my nature from my maker to be the light He picked for me. He calls me by my name.

Let it go. I am alive.

Amen!

September 4

You have said to me that You have every hair on my head counted. For the creator of all to have the precise detail derails any thought that I'm lost outside Heaven's trail.

This reality of my unique mark unites me with the greatest power ever to be.

When I am down, all I must do is comprehend His love and understand just how big God is. I'm reminded how intimately connected to my soul He is, which makes me whole. He has created me to be special. I humbly reflect on this one thought, which assures me for eternity. I am His, and He is mine from the beginning of time.

Amen!

September 5

God loves me, so, therefore, I can love others. This flow from creation's door fills me with the desire to be His love. So, I have to be free from thinking selfishly and see that He cares and provides for me. In this trust, I can gain the confidence to care and bear the difficulties that surround me. In every challenge, He calls me to be closer to my creator and sustainer. May I encourage the people I've come to know as they go to and fro and as we each grow to know You as Father and friend, who is always walking beside me.

In the valley, You call to me, and on the mountain top, You originate the glee and dance with me. Every challenge and triumph is a lesson to perfect my soul to know Your eternal glow, the original flow of love You gave to me. As I observe with Your eyes, I see magnificent potential in each soul You created.

Amen

September 6

I desire to surrender my ego that blocks me from embracing the soul You created for me. I desire this harmony with all Your children as one, a unity void of hierarchy.

You can calm my fears, insecurities, and mental gyrations just like You calm the sea. I am who You created, so may I accept Your gift of true life, as that is the ultimate lift. When I accept all You have given to me, You free me for love like a dove. As I release and let go of these mysteries, I can see every step was planned for me to grow as You led me.

Only when I am kind to myself can my heart be open for the blessings You've placed around me.

Amen!

September 7

God of Heaven, God of earth, God of my heart. You created all there is or is meant to be, including me.

I am in awe, even when I lack clarity, as You have made every star both near and far. You know everything that was meant to be, even the number of hairs on my head and my unique fingerprint.

I await for You to call all Your sheep to Heaven's gate. Let my story of lost and found unfold, always destined to return the peace from Your creation to eternal salvation.

I was Heaven sent to this time and place to live and grow in Your grace.

Amen!

September 8

Good God, my Lord, allow me to be the best of me, which is the miracle within. I've learned from man's distortions, the original sin. From the beginning, Adam and Eve, my old kin, were the start of our existence. But my sin contorts the perfection of You within me. After all, my origination comes from Your most awesome creation.

I'm not junk that smells like a skunk. It's Your appointment from Your anointing that makes me Your Heavenly creation. You came on earth as my savior to show all of us Your unconditional love. I walk in Your footprints and experience Your elation.

I'm here for Your purpose, perfectly planned. All I need to do is awaken and let You do the baking with no more faking. I don't have to worry about who to blame because it's You in me who will gain all the fame.

The nearer I walk to You, I'm protected and hear the beauty and majesty in all Your ways, like in Broadway plays.

Amen!

September 9

In my unconsciousness, I become mentally animal-like. Left to this animal nature asleep, I forget my true human nature. In this guise, I take on a disguise that I am less than I was created to be. I must awaken and stay above to experience the true nature of my very creator.

In the face of challenge, may my resolve and understanding grow, and may I truly know that Your way can never be truly thwarted. In me resides the everlasting light of creator, sustainer, and savior from beginning to end. You will transform me to the full glory of Your creation for all time to behold. You were, are, and always will be within.

Your wisdom is the loving spirit that constantly calms my spirit, calling me daily in every hour in a way I cannot humanly comprehend. Your wisdom is a loving spirit, whispering to me how I will eternally come to be. This is how I will come to know Heavenly immortality.

Amen.

September 10

Lord, may my Christian testimony be obvious in my work. Might I not fall prey to the order of the day, which tells me my views are superior, and my path and personal experience has led me to the only acceptable way.

This mentality divides and instills fear, creating a barrier that blocks me from seeing through the haze of selfishness. This prevents me from being Your love and compassion and from embracing Your greatest command to simply love You and love all the others. I can disagree and still be free, but only if I have love in my heart, just as You command. Routinely, I dismissed this core command and fell to the floor with fake claims of faith, promoting political philosophy as holy.

May I use my abilities to advance Your kingdom and not use Your kingdom to advance mere schemes of man for the illusion of power. Let my testimony of Godly living include respect and the ability to see You in those I differ from. The Holy Spirit might light the way, extinguishing utter confusion and hostile pollution. I lay down my weapon of consternation and rest in thee to be an instrument of peace with inspirational words that end the mire and unnecessary fire.

Grant my heart clarity to believe without being naïve that all Your creations are recipients of Your grace. Build bridges of unity in our human community, where consternation and egoic jubilation are surrendered at the sea and washed anew by thee in Your creation. Remind me that those I easily dehumanize for being on the other side actually have God inside. May I see Your ultimate purpose is to use me as a deliverer of Your love from above.

Amen!

September: Child of God

September 11

I am who God uniquely created for His glory. I am perfectly designed to meet the opportunities that He created for me. I have a daily divine appointment in the presence of the King of Glory. Every person I encourage and am encouraged by was arranged by HIM. The gifts that I receive and share were designed before the beginning of time with me in mind.

My God delights in His design and creation of who I am, where I am, and whom I'm with.

Everything. It's all by Him, known by Him, created by Him, designed by Him—for me!

Thank You, Lord, the God of love, the God who put my heart in place and instilled the breath in my being and put the light in my soul. Wow, the King of Glory is MY FATHER. I am His, and He is mine. He knows me by name, calls me friend, and even has the hairs on my head counted. Since this is true and God is for me, I guess I have nothing to do today but be filled with His glory, be powered with gratitude, and love all His people with the Love He created for me to share with You!

Amen!

_____
_____
_____
_____
_____
_____
_____

September 12

Lord my God, may I live in the reality, truth, and knowledge of belief in my total safety in You. Prevent all fears to exist, and may these lies disappear as they are only the illusions and stories in my mind. May my ego not pull me to the depths, but my spirit lift me to the heights of the Heavens.

Fear is interest on a loan I never took. I am free in the protective holy spirit. My reality is who You say I am, not who the world creates for me, but I am holy in Your sight, for You are holy, and You are the core of my reality, truth, and beauty.

I glow within as Your goodness, kindness, and light are the eternal truth. You are mine, and I am Yours. We fully delight in each other mutually as You are the creator, and I am Your created!

Praise You, my Lord and my God! Amen!

September 13

God is the Father of my heart. In the valleys, I cling to this truth as it is my only hope; there is no place to look but up. On the mountain peak, my ego deceives me, and I falsely think I'm my own creation. Then is the threat of separation, isolation, and depression in self-glory. I fall to the valley, only remembering the real truth when I delight fully in who I am in HIM. Here, I find peace, unity, joy, and elation.

I don't know how many times I'll need to return to the valley to be reminded that true, everlasting joy comes not from asking, "What or who am I?" but from knowing WHOSE I am! I am a child of God, was, is, and always will be!

Amen! Thanks be to God!

September 14

May my judgment not keep the river of grace from flowing through me to quench the thirst of my brother and sisters. May my soul consciousness awaken my core and be a ray of light to all I come to know.

Superiority and inferiority are both consequences of judgment. They funnel away the oxygen I have in the freedom of my faith.

May I surrender that suffocating judgment to the breath of Heaven. May I fully come alive and delight in the blessing I can be and the good I can do in creating a spirit of love, freedom, forgiveness, grace, and mercy.

May I drink freely from the fountain of my Father and delight in the one who provides all I need. As I stand in line for that fountain, which quenches all who thirst for the full freedom of forgiveness, I remember You uniquely and individually had me in mind as You breathed me into existence.

God made no mistakes EVER, so He didn't fail with me either. HlS quality control is unfailing and never in error, extinct, broken, or in need!

He's got me. He's got this! I only need to hang on to the hem of His robe.

Amen!

_____
_____
_____
_____
_____

September 15

Lord my God, You are the light within my being.
You are my courage that extinguishes the illusion of fear.
You are the source of all my joy.

My Lord, when I fixate on You, there is no depression, as guilt, shame, and grief melt into compassion, transforming into a passion for healing all the hurting I come to know.

Lord my God, You are love, and You live in me; therefore, the living love of God is the running river that flows through my veins.

Lord, WE are LOVE!

September 16

Lord my God, I rest in You. I am safe in Your presence. You lift my spirit and give me strength. I am grounded in Your truth. My hope rests upon You. I am what You intended. You created me to experience Your presence in this world and to be a reflection of Your peace. Lord, Your Godly grace has no end. I am as a child of innocence in Your mercy.

Amen!

September 17

Dear God, only You know the exact count of my days. Before the beginning of time, You decided when I would be on earth to do my work and decided when it would begin and end. When it rolls by, we often don't see it as special, precious, and irreplaceable as it is. The moments we have to encourage, bless, and inspire are appointments with destiny and represent the landmarks we leave behind upon those You gave us to love. I don't want to miss another moment of seeing the holy target and touching the hearts You gave me to be with.

It's not too late. I'm not yet with You in Your Heavenly home. I'm here to make the moments count for uplifting, enlightening, and being Your love on the earth You gave me to walk my journey upon. I'm still growing, learning, and forgiving myself. May I make the rest of the walk count for Your glory and reflection and be a glimmer in the hearts You gave me to save and love.

Amen!

_____
_____
_____
_____
_____
_____
_____
_____

September 18

God, I look to You for all I can do. Give me strength when I am weak. Give me a heart of compassion to see the hurting I can heal. May I console the lonely and be freed of the projection of fears that sidetrack me and keep me from bringing Your mercy to the people who immediately surround me.

Wither the deceptive illusions of the world that create arguments of separation. May I see that it's You within the hungry, hurting, lonely, or deprived.

May I become Your joy giver as You have been the source of mine. All I had or have to do is rely upon You and love others, growing to be free of judgment and comparison and simply love with the spirit You breathed into my soul.

Through Your power in me, may it be so! Amen!

September 19

Lord of grace, I lift my ear toward Heaven. I hear Your call to open my heart. May I be drawn to You. May I hear Your voice and discern clearly Your call to my spirit. Lead me today where You will use me to be an encouragement to those who need it. Allow me to have patience to listen before I speak. May I reflect who I am in You as others feel Your presence within me. Lord, allow me to see You in the souls of those I meet.

May this be a day that I grow in kindness and sensitivity to the surrounding souls, as I now see more clearly, it's You I see in them, and it's You they see in me.

Amen!

September 20

Open my eyes, Lord. Allow me to see Your miracles, majesty, and presence.

May I first see You in those I know, those I meet or simply greet.

May I recognize Your reality in those who are different from me. Help me see the love in the one before me, who is actually thee I see.

Just as I thirst to feel Your inner presence, so does my fellow man. They, too, need to be loved, surrounded, and called by their name, by You. Use my life to magnify Your call to peace, unity, and abundance.

Make my heart Your call to my neighbor, equaling my delight when Your presence is felt at their door as mine.

May our joy be as great for one another. Your love tears down the wall and creates harmony, unity, and true joy in knowing we are all one in the same, precious in Your name. Black and white, rich and poor, ill and well, Young and old, as to You these divisions are only illusions. Each soul is fully created by the mystery of Your breath and the creative construct of the mind of You, OUR GOD!

Thank You, my Lord, for perfect unity in Heaven. Now, I will work to make Earth a foretaste of Your Heavenly creation.

Amen!

_____
_____
_____
_____

September 21

My Lord, God, and friend, may my better nature rule within. Forgive me when I have betrayed this to conform and please others just to fit in.

May I freely and purposefully express the truth and goodness You breathed into me as an expression of You. May I know who I am in You. That I am enough, just as I am as You set in place upon this earth.

May I become NO ONE rather than becoming the one I've created, to be part of the crowd.

My fears drive me to appear as what I think will please others. But You are most pleased with the authentic nature and reflection of You that thrives freely in me, sharing Your glory that You desired me to be.

Too often, others settle for less than what You intended for them. They try to be worthy of their idea of others' expectations. But we are as special as grains of sand on the beach, uniquely perfect, different, yet equally precious.

May I fully welcome myself and my spirit's call for the inner beauty for which I was created by You. My deepest desire is to commune on earth the way the spirit of God has infused within me to ultimately walk with You in eternity.

Amen!

_____
_____
_____
_____
_____

September: Child of God

September 22

Lord, my heart, soul, mind, and body are anchored in You, my creator. The beauty of the day is provided by Your joy. The love from my pets is a reminder of the pure love authored by Your perfection. When I'm away and return home, the complete, resentment-free joy that I see in my dog reminds me of what it will be like for You to welcome me as I return to You in my eternal home.

I look to the sun, and the warmth on my face is an embrace of Your grace. I see the flight of a cardinal, and the mystery of the magic in its magnificence melts my annoyance. What could separate me from these constant reminders of love and the delight of life? In each of these created gifts, I'm reminded of the insignificance that I am and the magnificence You are.

Yet You set me in place, surrounded by Your constant calls to me. How could I ever doubt who You are in me? You are my amazing God of delight and perfect peace. May every step today be with the assurance that I'm coming nearer to home with You.

Amen!

September 23

God, I know when I surrender control to You, I free my soul to receive and know Your full blessing. Yet this doesn't always free me to let go of my tight grip on the illusion of my control. I remain attached to the desire to steer my ship.

But those moments I gain strength and loosen my grip are the moments You breathe air into the sails of my life, and You guide me further, faster, and smoother than ever before.

Wow! Your perfection, majesty, and precision amaze, excite, and guide.

May these moments grow and my control fade.

Might this magnificence remind me that You in me is greater than anything I could conceive.

May I grow in trust that I throw my hands in the air and yell with delight as I forever surrender the captain's wheel to the creator of all captains, for You are the creator of the ship of the universe in which You have placed me. You assure me that it is You alone who guides me to my eternal home.

Amen!

September 24

Wherever I go, I seek You—then I find grief transformed to peace. I find beauty in everything when my soul is focused on You. When I lose judgment for man, I see Your love in them.

When comparison fades to compassion, You are revealed in me, and Your reflection is in front of me. May I never lose the power of this clarity. Only the confusion of the story of my mind keeps me from true knowledge of Your filling of my heart.

Yesterday, now, and always, You are reminding me and calling me back to the comfort of this reality. With the innocence of a child, I ask You FOR EVERYTHING!

May my heart recapture this perfect and naive purity, knowing no brokenness, therefore fully open. I learned to close and protect my heart to the world's pain of disappointment and separation. If I can restore my childlike heart, knowing with certainty of Your protection, I can experience Heavenly inclusion and Your true presence. So, I call upon Your name, knowing You lift the dark clouds of earthly confusion if only I use the heart You gave me to hear.

Amen!

September 25

My God and my all in all, I so often think about that day that I will walk with You in Your physical presence in the Heaven I was born for. I've been earthly living but was always Heaven bound. I'm still at this weigh station with earthly reality in the meantime, but I'm beginning to ponder our first meeting. I often wonder what I will say, but now that I'm aging, I think I'll just let You talk first.

Will You ask where I lived, what I drove, or where I vacationed? With gray in my hair and a limp in my step, I now am sure it will be, "Did you live love fully, which was the greatest gift I gave to you? Did you have joy with the life I gave you? Did you love yourself as much as I loved you?

"Did you know you were ENOUGH? I just wanted my boy to be happy and close by. I made you just like me, wanting unity, community, laughter, and fun. All I wanted for you is what you, too, wanted for your very own sons. That's why I gave them to you, so you would glimpse understanding for the true delight I have in you.

"Did you leave a path for those I placed in your life to also meet me and hear with a glad heart that inspired them to enjoy the journey?

"Did you behold the natural beauty of the sea from the shore? Did you hike in my mountains, where I was waiting to whisper to you and look at the sky to remind you of my majesty?

"All these clues I left to comfort, encourage, and point you to my love for you.

"But you're home now, and all the anxiety that kept you from peace on earth will be understood by my grace, love, and delight, for you are my prodigal son."

September: Child of God

I can't wait for the embrace of my Father, who has been waiting for me at Heaven's door.

Amen!

September 26

I cast my cares on You, Lord.

You have told me I should. I know it, but so often, I attach to the misery of the problem and am unable to unleash it to You.

Somehow, I instinctively think that gripping the grime will solve it in time. Only releasing it to You in radical trust brings the freedom I seek. I lack the humility to just draw near enough to live in Your permanent protection. Grant me relief by giving me the trust of my place as Your child.

Bring me to the shade of Your awning of grace. Keep the dark clouds of the storm from descending.

May I understand it's just a second in time in the process of seasoning. I will come to understand that You've got THIS.

May I see the optimism and give gratitude rather than be unglued before it unfolds. When I am confused or brokenhearted, You are not, as You're in the midst of parting the clouds.

You are unveiling the sun's ray of warmth, hope, and Heavenly plans. The puzzle pieces are confusing, but when the whole picture is complete, I see there never was a reason to despair.

For I know that is how my story ends, but in the midst of the journey, let me glimpse the Heavenly miracles in store for this child of God.

Amen!

_____
_____
_____

September 27

Lord, might my soul awaken to the thrill of growing in Your glory. May my wisdom and understanding of You drive my core. May I exude righteousness from walking in Your light of truth. May the fruits of the spirit become my daily pursuit.

Might my ego become less and my zest for living from my spirit become greater.

Father, may I walk in the path of Your kindness.

I lack these qualities or even true desire for them, but my hope is You in ME. Through humility and desire for more of You in me, I am made new every day with a renewed chance to quench this thirst to be like You.

Apart from You in me, I cannot exhibit an iota of these things, but as Your child, I can be everything You have caused me to dream.

So be it, gracious and loving Father!

Amen!

September 28

Love created me, which is what I am in God's plan.
    Light, joy, and peace abide in me.
    May I release the pain within and return to the joy the world does not naturally contain.
    May Your strength, God, take the place of my weakness.
    Might I consistently make the choice between truth over illusion and You instead of fantasy in my mind.
    May I be an ally of You, God, and not my ego.
    May You display Your Love in me with those I know and come to know in the days You yet gift to me.

Amen!

September 29

May the deepest desire for peace rest in my heart, God.

Freedom is mine from You as there are no strings on me. The rays of Heaven keep me in place, the birds of the air are my symphony, and the sea my dance floor. Your gift to me is this earthly Heaven, earth!

To the extent it's up to me, may I project a call to harmony, good will, and kindness with earth and man, who You created to be in union and synergy.

Awaken me to know my energy precedes me in my words and deeds. May I have a calmness of spirit to greet those irrespective of the feelings they might be fighting and whatever haze they may be seeing through.

If I'm conscious and rest in You, I will project an approachability and loving kindness that allows them to see that it is You in me, allowing me to have a melting self-focus. Give me first a heart for others, in which I create the presence of Your blessing in the moment.

Create in me a heart that yearns for a community of graciousness, forgiveness, and understanding. Keep my ego from revving in response to every slight of a passerby, much less those I know who bring an instant reaction of hurt.

May I know that no one can hurt me when I stand on my own, leaning upon You.

Please free the one before me who can destroy my stillness with their own changing emotions.

May I be free to pause and rest in Your love and live to give the grace and mercy You freely serve to me.

Transform me, Lord, into Your earthly welcome door.

Amen!

Whispers From Heaven

September: Child of God

September 30

May I remember in each moment, Lord, that the people I meet might forget what I've said or done, but what remains with them is how I made them feel, just as Maya Angelou said. May this reminder from You and this awareness grant me a heightened sensitivity. May my soul dance in harmony with a desire to be a blessing to others I meet. I am blessed with this feeling of harmony and creativity to be a blessing as I was meant to be.

Amen.

OCTOBER: GOD'S PRESENCE

October 1

You are unchanging, constantly certain, predictable, and dependable.

My life is anchored and matters to you. You have told me to cast all my anxiety upon you.

So, with this in mind, I can observe and not absorb conflict, chaos, and trouble. Lord, keep me from this rubble.

God is within me, so where my feet pitter-patter matter.

May I have a sound mind and a healthy heart to start the day, remembering I always carry God within. May I stay on holy ground, overcoming the fray and keeping trouble away.

Amen.

October 2

Holy Lord, You are Holy! You are light, creating day even in every night. You are the direction within when I think I'm lost. Every fear waits for me to learn Your strength and security in the test that, with time, I will be fine. I fear only when I lose sight of Your presence. It's You who I'm tight with, who will fight the fright of any old night. So I rest my head when I go to bed because You are always right here and very near. I never had anything real to fear. My Holy God, Lord, and friend!

Amen.

October 3

I receive power when the Holy Spirit comes upon me. It reminds, renews, and strengthens me. When I think I'm depleted and at the end of my rope, You remind me I'm just being a dope. That's when You renew me and remind me whose I am. You are my friend who never leaves me and calls out to me, bringing me to bliss in eternity. In this, I am reminded I am free to follow thee.

Amen.

October 4

Lord, reawaken my thirst and creativity as You remind me that without a sense of humor, any paradise is hell without an awareness of my soul's connection to You, the creator, and without my deep love for other souls here and now. I risk the brisk reality of never really living, so may I be reminded to dare to laugh, love, and live . . . and I will! You have told me to ask, and You will give as long as I look up to You and humbly receive. Why do I so often forget Your recipe for my life's true prosperity? Heal me from the spiritual dementia that destroys a clear mind, and instead clear the path from my heart to the Heavens. When I gaze in the haze of distraction, remind me to remain in the fullness that You gave to me. I know now I must let go and trust You so I can fully be who You made me to be.

I'll use the time I have left to praise and follow You. So I stretch my hands out and just receive as I am deserving of the beauty You conceived.

Amen!

October 5

I no longer live, but it is You who lives in me! That is the wisdom I needed to be free.

For when I value this truth, I am able to love myself, ending my hostile thoughts and changing how I live. Just as You have first done, I will love myself unconditionally. Then my internal wall will fall and free the flow of love to all!

Before, I falsely followed mental distortions, thinking I was free when I was really in chains.

But now I am free in the safety and peace of God's eternal love!

Amen!

October 6

Everything I do is uniquely prepared by You. I don't always get it, but You do. So, I am patient as I grow to know You more. I am proceeding in the river's flow so that I might continue to grow.

This is Your perfect plan. With You, I face no false superiority or comparison, no hesitation to do what You have called me to do. All that negativity dissolves into the ultimate unity of love.

I'm a being of light reflecting Your kindness. I feel safe as I'm enveloped in the aura of Your presence. Past hurts turn into healing and growth thanks to Your promises. I pause to realize that in stillness, I can visualize the ultimate prize: life with You.

Amen.

October 7

May my life grow this day to have more of Your loving presence that tames life's mess to everlasting success.

Witnessing and discovering You inside takes away my pride. My spirit no longer hides behind shame. Faith allows me to freely share my true self.

Dissolve my guilt that hides my truest beauty. This gift of life You breathed into me hovers just below the veil. Your presence releases my soul to all that You are calling me to.

May I ride a spiritual surfboard through the high waves and experience Your glee in me. Magic happens just as I realize Your presence is in me.

Amen.

October 8

May my heart be pure, for my eye is on You. As I surrender myself to all my soul is meant to be, I'm spiritually free. My illusions kept me from resting in You. Now, I seek to be meek and follow You, even as the world around me tells me to be bold on my own. The first thing I can do to follow You is to open my spirit and connect us two.

What scared me as a man now comforts me as I am guided by You. I rest in my spirit with the joy of Your foundation of love. I rest in the stillness of Your simplicity.

Amen.

October: God's Presence

October 9

Lord God, I am always in Your presence. Yet I can only love if I see You in myself and others. With this in mind, I'll be able to stand the test of time as Your love reminds me it is You who's inside. The very breath I breathe is a reminder of how much You love me; You gave me this life for a reason.

So when I get lost in worldly concerns, and the dark clouds gather, all I have to do is see You in everything and return to You, my source of Love. By returning to You, I'm free from the lessons of life that I cut out with a knife. Your love is the lesson that repeats this feat until my soul is at Your feet.

Amen.

October 10

Draw me nearer to Your side, where love resides.
   Draw me nearer to Your side, desiring no place to hide.
   I can feed myself physically, but in Your presence, I am nourished in my soul.
   In this nourishment, I am led to assurance of my soul, which transcends my physical self. The joy You give is my strength and promise, found in our ability to love as You do, judgment-free.
   In this, every tear transforms into cheer!

Amen.

October 11

Remove my heart of stone from life's broken bones, disappointments, and misunderstandings. Give me instead a heart of flesh filled with Your understanding and compassion for fellow man. For You have said, the pure of heart see You. That is the truest promise that sees me through.

Emotions swing as circumstances bring different realities, but when I trust and rest in this promise, I am lifted as high as Your presence within. You are my perpetual friend who is always waiting for me. You change not. I remember just whose I am when I rest, trust, and feel the confidence of the full bloom of my soul.

I may forget Your presence, but when I catch my breath, You are always there. The air that fills my lungs wakes me up and fills me with Your presence. With Your voice filling my heart so clearly, I am in the presence of LOVE!

Amen!

October 12

My heart is open, and I live in trust, for my soul is well when it rests in You.

Make me all I can be by Your design. I am willing, and when I'm not, I'm willing to be willing.

The energy of Your love draws me. God's spirit is a magnet, drawing me today, tomorrow, and forever as I desire to be as light as a feather. Anyone who questions this in me cannot cause me to doubt. More than believing, I *know* Your presence surrounds me; I can feel it within me constantly. Just let it be the nature within me.

I do not need to tell others about this love. I just need to love them as You do.

The darkness of doubt has nowhere to go when my light is on. May You burn within me. All is well when I'm reminded God is always with me!

Amen!

October 13

My God and my Lord, You are adored. I can only live in this way connected to You today. Fear, insecurity, and jealousy are old liars, creating misery and false distance between You and me. I surrender these imposters!! These lower vibrations are false gyrations that create trouble in my interior bubble. I'm awake and alert, a new me saying goodbye trouble!

I cleansed my lens to release the accusations whispering within. As You draw me closer to You, You free me to know Your world that waits within me. What You have for me is better than the letter I write inside my mind. I listen to Your expressions inside instead of that silly voice in my head. You're in control, not me! The story I try to write only creates hostility. May worry be replaced with prayer as I let go and trust in You. I open my palms to Your control, here and beyond. Then, I am free to receive and experience what You give to me.

I release my worries about how I thought it should be because Your loving offer will all unfold as You told.

Amen.

October 14

May I melt fear with Your love. The proof that I'm not aloof is the light that reveals everything is alright.
 I remain still and at peace, realizing You are within. When I breathe, it's Your life force that is revealed. Your unconditional love never ceases, Your mercy never ends, and You greet me every morning to remind me Your presence dispels any confusion.
 In You, I find my rest from distress.

Amen.

October 15

I am blessed when I take refuge in the Lord. This awareness is my bridge from fear to Your love.

When I am awake and seek You, I'm restored. Every time I feel far from You, please whisper to me to come near. Now I can rest and resolve that I trust in You. I must release the emotions within that keep me from being the best Your spirit within called me to be.

Awaken my soul every day, for I am Yours, and You call to me in every difficulty. I am free to let go and take in Your promise of a new hope.

Amen!

October 16

You sent the Holy Spirit to descend upon me, guiding and teaching me so I could be gliding through life while lessening the strife. I rise above as each challenge calls me closer to thee. I can be a manifestation when I am in full gestation.

My greatest strength is my most vulnerable state, resting in trust and letting go of the lust for false security. I have more issues and tissues when I believe all is in my control. When I let go and trust what I should naturally know, You are the glue that makes my energy flow. In this, I fully know who and what You are as I am Yours. Your loving creation is perfection in the making. I delight in learning through my desperation, where You gain my full attention for the lesson of love and trust.

For You are the good shepherd of my soul!

Amen!

October 17

God, keep me from the contagiousness of other's grievances. May I not ride the wheel of others' resentment. May the words of my mouth encourage and project cheer instead of fear. I am enough. I am Your dear. I am in You, and You are the grounding of the truth of who and what I am. I am Your beloved.

Therefore, I will not attach to the confusion of the world or the meaningless act of hearing and repeating that which is below me. I am a projection of Your protection. I know it. I feel it. My every fiber and cell create a Heavenly vibration that transcends the world's excuses, which threaten to dim Your light in me. I am worthy of Your love. May I project and reflect that You and Your spirit and mine are one.

You are the source of everything. You are all, and You love Your creation and me. It's You who breathed life into me. As I mentally embrace and return to my breath, You urge me to lay down my strife, cutting it with a knife for a Heavenly life. It's Your reminder to me that You are before me, around me, and You surround me! I fly above the arrows of rage, resentment, complaint, and worldly jeers. For all I hear are the cheers of Heaven. My inner child plays, delights, protects, leaps before You, and keeps my sights on Your cradle. Your caress soothes my stress.

Cover me, protect me in these days of seeming insanity. In Your eyes, there is no blight, just inner light. Keep me confessing this blessing until my soul is fully finished here and is with You there.

I am awakened and alert to keep the light that You burn in me. I am a blessing. I've come here to use my gifts. May I catch myself before I wring my hands over the lack caused by public flack. Every step is guided by You, so why do the "boos" of another keep me from knowing this is Your world, and You have never lost control. All You need to do for this boy is let me take my joy in You!

I am protected, I am worthy, my mind no longer takes flight but rests in Your delight.

Amen.

October 18

I will keep my heart open and experience the delight of the full presence of God.

I am just one piece of God's jigsaw puzzle. The incredible mystery is I've found all the other pieces that surround me. I don't need a muzzle as I sing while experiencing this puzzle. My life reflects this glee I feel. He sees me in His grand unity of mankind; all I need is to WAKE UP, receive, and believe.

I fit together with all those I see, and they are a perfect fit with me. That's a different kind of fit. The world's illusions and deception constantly pulled me into lower energies, its creepy calls catching me when I was no match. I was concerned with what I thought others just might be thinking of me.

But I can breathe and detach from this harmful mindset, experiencing the light without blight as all enemies take flight. I can flush that which is less than I'm meant to be. The anger around me is no longer the poison whose syllables ring in my ears. Now, when I allow God to speak through my heart, I can start to be just as free as His spirit instills within me.

My soul can now dance on earth without the time in purgatory. All I need to do is filter the insanity that created a lesser me than HE created me to be! I am a powerful and worthy person. God's plan rests peacefully in HIS creation. I just needed to be freed of the negativity of man-made creation, for HE IS THE REAL THING!

That's a BIG DEAL, and I reel with delight for what is real AND everlasting in me, calling me to just receive and BE!

Amen!

Whispers From Heaven

October 19

Lord, free me from negativity, collect up all the accumulated stories from dark creativity. I lift my open hands to receive the light from Your spirit, which erases darkness for the richness of You as the sky above me is all blue, and that's true.

Life was not meant to be in strife, but I often think it's so thick I can cut it with a knife, and it occasionally makes me as cold as ice. But my set point is NICE!

May my earthly habits be cradled in the feelings of being at home with You. I hold onto the memories of You in me because that's who I'm always with . . . You! I'm not waiting, performing an audition or hoping I'm deserving or good enough. You made me to be at home with You from my first earth breath.

I've learned fear here, but it's just false evidence appearing real. Now that I've learned to be still, I breathe again and believe in Your goodness and acceptance. I'm a sparkle in Your eye just like a star!

Amen!

October 20

God, I receive Your divine goodness. It creates Your wonders within me. All my needs are met in You. I am cradled and surrounded by Your love. Your call for Your will is within, for You placed it there at the moment of life. It is Your desire for me to shed struggle and delight in receiving Your love and abundance in Your wholeness and to share it with Your people.

In this, I delight in Your presence. Everything works for my good by trusting Your will and guidance. Wars in the world are man's distance from wholeness in You. Peace from Your wholeness and harmony is mine through my surrendering to You. Give me a deepened trust in You, leading me to the alignment with You that turns turmoil into peace and worry into joy.

Deepen my strength of surrender to fully trust in Your goodness. I know that You are on the throne of grace, life, and eternity, for all those who sit at Your feet to receive Your promises of purity, peace, and everlasting joy desire this rest in You.

Peace. Shalom.

Amen!

_____
_____
_____
_____
_____
_____
_____

October 21

I am enough. I am whole. I am Yours, my Lord.

Everything I do now enables me to be cloistered in who I am in You: protected, cared for, and experiencing Your harmony. Therefore, everything is a privilege, and nothing is a struggle. In Your lessons, there is growth and comfort, and I'm expanding and ultimately experiencing nearness to You.

You call me by name, and every day, in every way, the goodness of You, God, is present inside of me. You allow me to see the good that at first, I do not see. Once I look through the eyes of the spirit within my being, the answers to my questions are revealed. My confusion turns to clarity. Even the world's chaos becomes my comfort as You surround me and protect me with a shield of Your peace. Remembering who I am in You transcends who I'm perceived to be in the world.

May Your presence become more powerful in me this day.

Amen.

_____
_____
_____
_____
_____
_____
_____
_____
_____
_____

October 22

Lord, I feel Your presence. It brings me the deepest joy. It girds me in a strength that breeds the courage from Your kingdom. May my prayer be music to You as my soul sings in the understanding of Your presence. There is no fear, doubt, or worry when I feel the presence of Your holy spirit.

May my life be an unceasing prayer as I come into Your joyous love. All is well, no matter the worldly circumstance. Heaven is Your promise to me as I trust and rest in You.

I live to give You gratitude, for that alone brings laughter to my soul and joy to my heart. Resting in this day is a joy as it is one day nearer to being in Your everlasting presence.

Amen!

October 23

Lord, may my days on earth be an expression of my soul. Might my soul rest in Your peace as it is the indwelling of You in me on earth. Might the illumination of the Holy Spirit's warmth be ever-present and surround me. Tame my instinct to compare and judge as I wish not to be judged by others. May my judgment evaporate and transition to loving-kindness.

Cause my spirit on earth to dance. Allow my steps to be with the confidence of a child of the king. May we accept and receive all circumstances of life with the assurance of trust and faith in You, as You have placed earth on its axis, and nothing is beyond Your will and control.

In Your Heavenly order, confusion turns to logic, chaos to peace, trauma to rapture, and even my grief grows to become a highway to the deepest spiritual journey of healing. May my experience fuel an empathy that I may offer to others. May I comfort others in the way I need to be comforted. May our mutual compassion create harmony.

May I learn what I lack and unlearn that which I thought I knew but confuses and causes me to see less clearly than You designed.

May I fully rest and feel the fullness of Your presence . . . Lord my God!

Amen!

_____
_____
_____

October 24

Because You are fully present in every moment, I am whole. Harmony reigns because of the beauty of Your wholeness. I have all I am because of all You are. I am Your wholeness, which gives me the privilege of being Your hope. Healing is happening in me because I'm being peace, harmony, and abundance to Your children because of Your wholeness in me.

May Your wholeness of presence call me when I become distracted. When I forget who I am in You, I become enabled to be Your love. When I stumble, pick me up; when I forget, remind me; when I am distracted, call my attention to the wholeness in You that melts all separation. But in unity, use me to provide Your very own Heaven-sent wholeness as You have sent to me a gift beyond treasure, and it was free to me by the humility of acceptance.

I call upon You, Lord, for I know with certainty that You are near. May I reclaim it every hour of every day.

Amen!

October 25

God of grace, grant me compassion that allows me to understand that which I do not.

Deepen my desire to understand more than to be understood.

Speak to my heart when I attempt to convince others of "facts" I have learned when I simply need to be more addicted to understanding and learning than teaching and persuading. May the cracks in my head bring light to my heart of understanding.

Those victories of persuasion that created distance from my brother are victories in my head and a defeat for my soul.

May unity be strengthened and I be used to share Your Love beyond the memorization of Your word.

But through my life, You unfold.

May my life resemble more of a love letter than a rule book.

May my heart be just as open to a stranger as it is to my own sons.

May Your own grace, mercy, peace, and love minimize ME and MAGNIFY You within.

Amen!

October 26

Lord of Heaven, creator of earth, creator of my soul.

Your peace rests within as I seek and lose the stories of my mind for the peace of my inner being.

Your peace permeates when I rest fully in You in this moment.

There is nothing but stillness in my soul as You center my reality of earth and Heaven. I do not suffer when I cement my mind, body, and spirit in the truth of Your presence right now. You anchor my existence, which is the foundation of perpetual joy. Peace is magnified in my core as I trade the stories of my mind for the truth of Your spirit's fullness in this moment.

You are the one I trust, for You created me to experience the wholeness of being in a constant state of Your presence.

Wow, awesome God. I was made for Your pleasure. What a privilege to live in a constant state of Your full presence! May Your holy spirit guide my life, leading me to the perfection of Your presence!

Amen!

October 27

My weakness becomes strength in the Lord. My sadness becomes joy submitted to Him. My Blessings are magnified in His goodness. I overcome fear when I view it all from the Lord's perspective, and courage abounds.

Yet an instinctive fear within has defied the wisdom that would be gained by silence, serenity, and simply being alone when only You are with me. Why do I fear this? It is only in the quiet that You can whisper to me without the interference of man-made noise. I can now comprehend Your peace.

This will allow me to grow in wisdom and understand the language of Heaven.

I am ready to know, appreciate, and grow in the silence of God that nourishes my soul and feeds my mind.

There is nothing that separates me from the goodness, grace, and mercy of my Lord. In Him, all things are made new.

Amen!

October 28

I am a child of God, desiring to experience Your pleasure. I allow my own creation to cloud the one true creation of Father God. Mine is a temporary illusion that leads to the pain of separation, as constant motion creates commotion, giving the benefit of sedation. This is the earthly imposter of serenity. God's is Heavenly and a permanent place of peaceful perfection.

In this world, I've worked so hard to be noticed, but in healing, I now know invisibility, where I can find transparency. In this, I can be still, alone, quiet, and delighted in the intense light I was meant to be. His power in me holds me in His hands, truly free and at rest.

No show is required, and command performances have ceased. Now I'm learning that just resting in His presence creates the greatest peace on earth as it is in Heaven to come!

Amen.

October 29

You are my constant peace and presence. I just need to receive and believe Your Spirit.

You guide me in the night, and I am in full delight when my mind no longer goes in flight.

I can tame this frailty when I'm awake and aware. It's then I feel grounded and surrounded with all Your glory, as today is my new story.

With renewed energy, I embrace the joy found in Your presence within me.

Amen.

October 30

Refresh my soul and rejuvenate my mind as I learn to lean upon you. May I lay down those things that create the bumps in the road on my highway to heaven. The journey through the land takes on highs and lows from life's living flows. I feel you beside me every step of the way. You call to me incessantly.

Amen!

October 31

God is the breath of life. His breath through us is love infinitely eternal.

The stillness of my mind proves the presence of God in my soul.

The beauty of His spirit is my force of life.

My spirit rests in the wholeness and permanence of my Lord.

The gift of my life is from You, my creator.

God is ever-present and always moving my spirit closer to His own. This is for my highest and greatest good.

My delight is in the truth of my never-changing God. He is always moving for the growth of my good and His goodness. Always moving but never changing. He now resides in me as I remain still and fully receive His glory. It intoxicates my soul and enlivens my spirit. This perfection consumes me as I walk nearer daily to His perfection, presence, and everlasting Peace and Praise!

Amen!

NOVEMBER: THE GIFT OF LIFE

November: The Gift of Life

November 1

Everything is possible, for I believe in You. My faith makes this true. I don't have to be upset, for if I set my mind on You, it eliminates the grind. It's a whole new find when my heart starts and rests in who I am in You.

Today is met with a new bet on love that paves the way for this worldly stay.

Amen.

November 2

Faith, hope, and love. Might these three be the trilogy swirling around me.
For all of these bring me close to thee.
As I walk in this world, and I'm caused to blink when I think things lesser than me; I can wink when I remember and think on these: faith, hope, and love.
This is all I need to remain sustained. Now, I give everything to gain as I am free from all blame.

Amen.

November: The Gift of Life

November 3

Lord, I am here and am wondering why. Why can life be so hard? If it's Your gift to me, why does it challenge me? The days can be hard and filled with fear that I can hardly bear. Yet I know You care. In my discomfort, I look up to You and ask—are You really here? It's then I feel You, and I resolve to carry on and follow You.

Just when I can't walk along, it's then You carry me in. My human valley is when I call to You through it all, preventing me from a fall. When I'm frustrated and think I'm through, You are there and have been all along. With Your comfort, I sing a song of praise. So when I'm fired up or just plain old tired, there You are. I open my eyes to see clearly that all of it is Your constant call to me. Now, my mission is to live for You above.

Amen.

November 4

Help my unbelief to know that I am welcome at the table of grace and that I deserve healing and reconciliation.
    For You have not given me conditions for Your grace. You created me for a relationship with You. May I soar as an eagle with wings, constantly looking to You and dreaming of everything You planned for me. May I touch those You have surrounded me with. May I humbly learn from those You gave to encourage me. I pray we will carry on fueled by the grace in this space.
    The gleam in my eye and the spark in my heart represent all You do in and through me. I hope to remain strong and always carry on, for where there has been no struggle, there is no strength. In every circumstance, You have benefited me to be Your grace, love, and mercy, which is my ultimate strength and will see me through anything.

Amen.

_____
_____
_____
_____
_____
_____
_____
_____
_____

November 5

If God is FOR me, then who could be against me? Life is a gift, and You put everything in order, even if I can't always see it.

So I shall remain awake and experience the gift of it all. I'm learning that control of what I say and do and how I invest my gifts are this gift of free will from You. If I'm about to drop the ball, You pick it up before it can fall. I let go and trust You.

The only real lesson of life is to keep trusting You. I imagine myself running into Your arms, preventing that feared fall and dissolving my doubt to trust. You're always there, waiting for me with open arms.

Amen.

November 6

You prepared in advance the good work I would do, for I am Your handiwork made in You. When I ponder this, I rest knowing that I'm not just a random event, happenstance, or mistake. You made me with Your very own hand with purpose in mind, and it starts when I'm kind. In this assurance from You, I find peace and gratitude for all You have equipped me to do. This path that I've found creates a synergy that touches others' lives, energizing me to be alive, not just mildly satisfied.

I know exactly what to do when I slow my mind to recharge in You. Today is a gift to give others a lift because it's a boomerang of joy to celebrate as Your boy.

Amen!

November 7

My joy is from my spirit; protect me, guide me as I learn to let the spirit lead in place of my ego, which only ever brought misery. My ego and my spirit are polar opposites. My spirit calls and calms me, opening my eyes to see You and Your grace. You created my spirit, but my ego is my own man-made madman, hell-bent on separating me from You. I will never be denied the beauty of who I am in You—it was always meant to be!

So, in clarity, I see! I am and was always meant to be Your friend, child, companion, and eternal blend.

Amen.

November 8

In You, I am complete. Since You created me, peace has always been waiting in my soul.

Your spirit is persevering, always whispering that You, the source of my peace, never leaves me.

As long as I am breathing, I can be free of worldly stress, for You are waiting patiently to remind me that You are the giver of life. Lord, keep calling me to open the eyes of my heart so I can be grounded in You from the start.

Amen!

November 9

It is well now, always, and forever. May God give me the ability to see this truth with total clarity.

I am anchored in You, pointing myself and others to Your kingdom. My human mind wastes time pondering the lesser things. But when I simply open my heart and take the time to listen to you, You lead me into gentleness that transcends the worldly mess. May I share Your light with those around me, using my humanness for good as long as I am anchored in You.

Now, I'm ready to meet the day to see who I can fortify.

Amen!

November 10

Jesus wept. Not by emotion but by empathy. Not fear but love. The tears are healing, not helpless. The weeping is a call for me to be comforting to myself and others. There is no hopelessness in the end of times, so may my mind be transfixed on the promises that make me as new as each sunrise in each new day. In the world around me, I see who and what I was meant to be—part of Your blissful creation. So if I can accept, conceive, and expect this, I can be free.

As I empty my worldly mind of its false images, I become like the caterpillar transformed into a majestic butterfly. I am a new creation in Christ, able to fly way up high.

Amen!

November 11

Lord, might I be so light that I feel my soul is taking flight. It is right for me to reflect Your light when I'm in Your full delight. After this earthly plight, I surrender the fight and gain access to Your full light.

The realization of Your plan for humanity is now clear to me.

You gifted me this eternal soul to ride high and not be lost. The plights are only from my illusion, as my fight for superiority is just my confusion. I see with gratitude all the gifts You gave me. They fit perfectly to share with those around me.

My human body is temporary, but my permanent mission is the eternal perfection of my soul. Might You constantly remind me of my purpose here on earth before Heaven welcomes me home. Your eternal mission is my truest commission.

Amen!

_____
_____
_____
_____
_____
_____
_____
_____
_____

November 12

Lord, maximize in me a real ability to recognize and be at home in my soul. In this reality, my soul delights in the lights of Heaven in the here and now.

I no longer would call out for Your kingdom to come, for Your will is already done. The soul within already makes me whole, conquering that pitiful made-up troll. Nothing prevents me from the full delight in the seat of my soul.

My ego can hold on and project my human exterior, but it's only my soul that is eternally Your kin. To be out of the body is for my soul to be returned to You, healed from an earthly flu.

I am no longer held back by the blues, for my spirit is humanly awakened. My path to a permanent soul is to awaken and bring Heaven's light in full flight so I can delight today. On this day, I don't need to go hither and yon! Because eternity starts now, not hindered at all. As my soul is whole RIGHT NOW, no longer awaiting a casket call, my spirit is always alive and well!

Amen!

November 13

I cannot escape death, but I can escape fear of it. To set the mind on the flesh is death, yet to set the mind on the spirit is peace. Wow, this is the decision left to me.

God's love is in me. May I be complicit in that energy that reveals You fully in me. May I see it. Be it. Believe it. Show it. Because I deeply know it.

May I be contagious and experience the joy of imitating You and imparting Your very energy to those I see!

May the rest of my life grant progress toward this measure in me. The happiness of the flow I know is a big thing, which I master by small steps, and my soul jumps for joy.

In this season of life, I choose to create rather than berate, surrendering challenges to my soul in harmony with Your nature in me. Amen!

November 14

Trials come and go, but I remain in the healing of Your love. You have assured me the crown of life by loving You. That prevents me from ever feeling like a clown with a frown.

I am upheld from the moment I wake. From head to toe, I have had a glow from Your energy flow since I began to grow.

Don't you know I just had to stop traversing to and fro because the whole time, I'm here below. I now reach and grow to the highest Heavenly heights I can see.

So my love is within me from birth to bodily death, as from beginning to end, my soul was never going to offend. This real part of me lives to eternity because my soul has no end!

Amen!

November 15

May Your grace and peace be my front line of protection.

Allow these eyes to see Your glory. On my own, I see what is gory.

But when I allow You in me to be free, it is as You meant it to be to call me to see through Your eyes of love. I am lifted to the Heavens when I practice being and seeing You within. So remind me that You are always before me. You never abandon me; even when I forget, You're always there.

Protecting, leading, guiding me is what I must remember every day.

Amen.

November 16

God, have mercy on me. May my compassion grow and my anger be depleted. May I see more clearly through Your eyes that soften my heart, opening me to forgive others and myself. In this reality, I finally feel the freedom from guilt that You have already designed for me. I am no longer blocking the flow of compassion and charity.

May I deepen my trust in You, allowing my soul to grow.

May I reflect Your grace to those I know so Your love will freely flow.

For you are before me in all circumstances, guiding me to live as You've called.

Amen.

November: The Gift of Life

November 17

My Lord's gift of life unfolds just as You told. When resting in whose I am, I'm free to be who You created me to be: whole and free, delighting in the God-made, only accepting the man-made. Like a blade of grass is simple but shows God's majesty, I will be glorious in the God-made.

My journey off this perfect path created turmoil that You allowed me to choose through all that confusion and booze. But awake, I'm free to rest fully in THEE! When I thought it was up to me, I traversed far from Your great northern star. But I awake and reckon that Your freedom and joy were always available to me at my beckon.

So I awake this day with Your reality alive in me; I am free. The experience of life from a healed mind, where anxiousness melts to hope, fear to love, and toil of work to my purpose from God.

When the Bible tells me to be anxious for nothing, it is only to be if I let go of ME. My mind, body, and soul are healed from the traumas of life when I accept You and let go of what is not intended for me. Healing, I now know, is awareness and acceptance. This actually makes this instruction not only achievable but realized as God's initial gift to me.

Thank You, my Lord!

Amen!

_____
_____
_____

November 18

The reason God made me was so He can love Me! I celebrate that by loving others and magnifying His love. I hold tight to His light as that's the way to bring about His light even in the darkest part of night. It's not trite but oh so right to chase away the fright with grace and Heaven's might. So, fear is a flawed state of mind that is not kind. A thought out of control only has to be told no, for I am not my mind but an observer to its whims and pleasures until I awaken to who and what I am.

I am enough, just as God has created me to be. His very own love permeates me and is joyous and peaceful, like a dove with my highest calling from above. My state of mind is not on autopilot, as my spirit is my eternal elation when it's my navigation.

So be it. So it is.

Amen!

November 19

God of Heaven, Lord of Earth, King of truth, and Purveyor of reality. You are the author and creator. I am writing on the pages what You dictated.

I can only know total peace when I rest in the perfect understanding that I am Yours. All events were created for me to know, grow, and delight more in You. So, with this day, whether it brings sadness or gladness, I will rest and delight in who I am in You and in the growing knowledge that my trust is expanding in this indisputable truth. I'm just as You designed, created, and set in place, and the only true God in the universe delights fully in me, HIS creation, for I was created by the master of creation!

Amen!

November 20

Lord, work in my heart of love for You to overpower my mind when it is far from You. Take my feet on a Heavenly path when worldly pursuits that impress man tempt them away from Your will. Forgive me when I'm weak, and the desire to impress, please, appease, and conduct showmanship for approval are overcome by the simplicity of serving You.

May serving You overcome my mind's desire to impress man as Your voice draws me away. When my ego desires the stage show to receive applause, might I instead be drawn to my knees to serve You by filling the needs of others.

Might I develop a kinder heart toward the homeless rather than seeking the approval of the powerful. Give me eyes to see the goodness I can do and share the inspiration of Your grace. Might my trust in You give me Your provision of abundance and erase the fear of scarcity that keeps me from compromising. I am who You say I am. I am whom You authentically and uniquely created. This alone makes me good enough. Therefore, I need nothing more.

Clear the clouds of confusion that are not for Your glory but are simply the power of man. Unlock my jaws to speak of love over war and unity over chaos. May division and confusion for the sake of worldly power plays give way to the healing of man's heart and will to love You first and love others as myself. Forgive my sins and give me a clean heart, oh God. May Your will be done in my soul.

Amen!

_____
_____
_____

November 21

Lord, allow me to see this world through Your eternal lens. When I only see the immediacy of today, I can lose sight that I have an eternal timeline. When I rest in the reality that man's timelines are our own construct and not created by You, I can breathe, smile, and approach others with an open heart and not a hurried mind. My hurriedness becomes self-importance that blinds the love within and hides You, the light within me.

When I see eternally, I am not in too much of a hurry to be kind. Short-term problems turn into long-term lessons.

I just need to remember You gave me forever. No one is a distraction but an opportunity to practice love, charity, and understanding.

Short-term hurried living is a poison. No one in a hurry is loving. It robs me of the realities of others and makes me self-absorbed.

When I'm in a hurry, victory is often paid by the price of galvanizing the hostilities and judgments among mankind. This is an empty victory, and it will not last into eternity!

Lord, give me the freedom of eternal rather than short-term thinking. After all, we have forevermore!

Amen!

_____
_____
_____
_____
_____

November 22

Freedom is not a legal status granted me but a mental state of reality that's a gift from God.

I am who God breathed into life. I have learned my freedom is in who I am, just as He said I will be. Thank You, God, for life and my liberty.

May I be an extension of You, uncorrupted of this world and its seeming reality.

You alone have ordered the days and created in me a heart of love, life, and Your very energy.

I work with joy, knowing Your purposes for me are within me.

I rest in You, which brings me vibrancy and vitality to do as You have willed for me.

I surrender the constraints of striving to create a self that I conjured as necessary to be acceptable to others.

You alone created me to be as I am for Your pleasure.

Amen!

November 23

May I glow with the spirit of the Lord. Guide me by Your leading, God, to delight in charity and lead with humility.

May I overcome evil with good feelings, making me nauseous at the first thought of revenge, score-settling, or grievance-holding.

May the light of Your presence wash away any desire of war and separation with my neighbor, friend, workmate, or relative.

Cause an energy of delight in living with and owing love to each of these.

Transform my heart through Your spirit, so my primary language is the law of love.

May I know definitively, as You have promised, that I can overcome evil with good.

Give me a spirit to serve and wait upon You, my Lord!

Amen!

November 24

We were called to freedom to serve through our love from You, Lord. The strength I have is You in me.

May I be filled with Your energy of love to bring light to darkness. May I provide Hope where there has been struggle.

Because of Your grace and forgiveness, may this reality fuel my ability to deeply love and forgive those who hurt me. Let me see from Your eyes when I am too self-focused on my wounds to not be equipped to freely love my enemies.

May Your wisdom fill me with a thirst for goodness and kindness.

Might You avail me this day to place You in my heart in such a way that I'm drawn to be understanding to those who hurt. Inspire my sensitivity to the needs and broken hearts of those I meet. Might Your loving kindness wash the anger of the world.

Allow me to see You every hour of every day, so I am reminded of whose I am and who I am a reflection of.

Amen!

November 25

Loving You, God, allows me to love all Your people in Your power for Your purposes. I am only an empty pipe for Your fuel of love to pass through.

Lord, allow my heart to be louder and my mind to be quieter.

Allow me to forgive so freely that I forget even HOW to judge and compare.

Let me let go of the past, living in the present, and trusting You completely for the future.

May I be a fountain of a supply of Your endless love! I came from love and go to love, then life is just what I AM between these. Lord, help me to choose love between.

Loving You allows me to love all Your people with Your power and purpose. I am an empty pipe for Your fuel of love to pass through.

Amen!

November 26

God's Spirit dwells in me! His love, His gifting, His calling are within.

A creative act is an expression of love, an expression of who God's indwelling in me is.

When I feel lost, I'm reminded I am found by whose thumbprint is on my heart. My Lord is the drummer to my heart's beat.

When my eyes are in alignment with Heaven's rays, it illuminates delight.

Euphoria then vanishes struggle and unleashes God's love within.

The highway to Heaven is paved in such a way that my feet are cushioned with each step.

When my physicality is outweighed by the truth of my spirituality, I am free to fly like the eagle!

I am Heaven's bird, mightily soaring yet adoring the sweetness a hummingbird craves.

May my Lord allow me to be so high and yet so sweet in His presence now and always.

May I be His light to make the path clear, clean, and easy to follow for all those I know that He gave me to be with now and for always.

Amen!

_____
_____
_____
_____
_____

November 27

The highway to Heaven is through my heart; the accelerator is my soul as it revs in reverence to my God.

But the highway to hell is in the false deceptions as the circles of my mind create a false illusion.

The jumper cables connecting me to others that bring unity, harmony, and alignment are always available. The danger is in the potholes, which are the lies I listen to and hold onto. In these lies, I find only the arrogance of judgment, the poison of comparison, and the destruction of self-centeredness that only strangle, isolate, and never define my plight.

I am truly a creation of the one true, living God who created me. Therefore, my life is joy the way God planned it to be. When I fully realize this by nullifying the ruminations of the mind, the lies fade for the beat of my heart's drum that is in tune with the rhythm of Heaven. There is just JOY waiting for me, as the rest was just a lie.

Amen!

November 28

You left Your word that promises me that You are the Spirit, and where the Spirit of the Lord is, there is my freedom.

When I'm less than You gifted me to be, I am a mere prisoner in my own mind.

May I not be temporarily blind and find freedom in every day. It is, after all, what you say! I am above the worldly mental fray.

I awake and say HEY, I am free on this new day for the peace You have left in me. But it's my choice to be free and accept what You say.

I choose to be lifted up. When anything threatens this, I return to my breath to be reminded to surrender to Your true love! You give me this freedom of life, now and forever.

Amen.

November 29

My hope is in You. When I fully comprehend who You are, this hope is enough!

It is all I need to be eternally secure, not just in my moments of doubt. This allows my soul to smile with all assurance and creates stability in my frailty.

For You made me for each moment in time that I'm physically living through. In a world of trauma, Your hope in me is everlasting and true. My permanent reality of hope is what sees me through the peaks and the valleys of all You expose me to.

All that challenges me is my opportunity to be renewed in this hope I have in You.

I am grounded in this truth You have given me—that my hope is in You.

Amen.

November 30

It's me, Lord! But You already know!
You're the one who formed me in my mother's womb. You already knew all the roads I would go. You call and lead me in all You had already planned for me. You have all the days accounted for, knowing when I'd stay the course and fall to my own source. Always calling me back and never tiring to meet me again and greet me with Your restorative love all the way from above.

You have never left me alone, especially on the grayest of days. When the bluest of skies would peek at me, I could feel Your great majesty. You are my loving, eternally living father in all ways and all times, keeping track of me. I am Yours, and You are mine all of the time, even when I do things that aren't fine. It's then You remind me that even You can grieve for those You made and always cherish.

Then You allowed me to be a father so I myself would know Your own true love.

For You are my Father, and I know deep in my being that You love me so.

Amen!

DECEMBER: TRUST

December 1

As I learn from the darkness, I experience the light. You erase the fears of the night.

Trust and faith comfort me because fear and love can not coexist, and fear is no match for God's unconditional love. As I surrender to this love within, fear dissolves like Jello in a hot tub.

In dark times, I find the courage that allows me to receive the light.

I say so long to fear from any dark night as that is a made-up plight that falls to God's sustaining light.

Amen!

December 2

Love dissolves the bad habits that limit my mentality. My power, strength, and worth are stronger when I give thanks for this gift of life. So why does my mind teeter on the brink of lesser things? I forget just whose I am as doubt comes in. But I am who You say I am . . . Your beloved, Your child, which makes me complete enough as I am!

Amen.

December: Trust

December 3

I ask, I seek, and I know I'll find, just as You have told me I will. For You have filled my very being with the knowledge that You are here with me. You sustain and guide me all of the days to grow to know You more. My doubt is not about fleeting moments as it finds no binds when I rest in the promise of seeking You. I replace my self-rebuke as it is just a fluke. I was created to live in glee and be free from consternation, self-judgment, and damnation.

It's when my heart is open and seeking the freeing sensation of simply knowing You deep down in my soul. I don't need a stage, just an open heart from the start. To quench self-doubt from the truth of what You're all about.

How can I be self-condemning when all I need to see is that I'm free. All I need to do is just BE!

Amen!

December 4

I do not know how to make the world glow. But when I empty myself of my ego, I seem to grow spiritually. I receive the flow of the spirit. It fills me, and I follow the prayer that comes to me. As I empty myself of the world's complexities, I receive Heaven's serenity as the spirit Himself intercedes for me. So the less of me, the more of Him. It becomes simple and puts a dimple on my face in place of disgrace.

All I need is to fully accept His grace right here in this place.

Amen!

December 5

Forgive me for each time I ever used Your word in an attempt to gain superiority. You provided it to me to share Your love and not be used as a license to condemn or a tool to destroy.

For You are THE WORD! Your word is a love letter. I just need to read, receive, and believe.

But so often, in my diligence for relevance, I used it as a tool of division, separating, and declaring my own superiority.

May I simply receive it and be transformed by Your love, not for my appearance of performance but JUST BECAUSE. When I believed I was in control, I lost sight that it's Your might bringing me pure light.

For it's Your love that builds up and does not destroy or tear down by the power of Your crown. After all, it's You who told me to love all the others around me.

Your power uplifts me and causes me to delight, which is how I chase away all fright with Your might, bringing light.

I choose to submit, freeing me of the thought that control is mine. For You know just the way I should go, and You whisper to me so! In this, I surrender my control to Your outcomes.

Thank You, Lord. When I remember just who You are and that You're my truest and trusted friend, I'm free with nothing to prove, provide, or advise. I'll be an example of Your perfection, giving no others rejection.

Just love!

Amen!

December 6

You alone are my significance and all the affirmation I need. It's only when I forget this that I create my own misery. When I rise above and am reminded, I fly beyond the sky when I set my mind on what's way up high. Up here, problems are possibilities, and Your light of love creates perfect holy unity.

In this, I learn to cherish uncertainty as it's the beginning of this unscripted journey to diminish fear. I'm now in Heaven's gear. Your love dissolves all fear.

Amen!

December 7

Courage is not false bravado where my ego performs.

It's submission, allowing all fear to be cast in the fire of my healing. Because when I cry out to You, You are there faithfully. You said You'd never leave, and You stand by Your word. I can conceive of all Your promises made for me, so my God, my God, I need You now; You are the rock of all ages. You planted me for Your greatness, so I call on You, who made me courageous. I can be fearless! My redeemer lives, leads, and loves.

I need You always, and I am now standing on the rock of Your faithfulness.

You are the same in the days of Moses and the same God for me now!

Amen!

December 8

Thy will be done on earth as in Heaven.
Something wondrous is always happening—God is fully present in me. So, I have every reason to be through with this human flu that turns me blue. As what is new is Holy brew. It's His loving presence alive in me and in all of creation. He expresses His love perfectly in and through me. So may my humanity give way to my eternal spirituality. God and I, in wholeness and harmony, are ONE. His light guides me in any dark tunnel, for His might ends false fright from any night. I attach to His promises and let go of all passing emotion. The Spirit's plan is for me to know all is well and everything is working for my highest good.
I am Your beloved, in whom You are well pleased.
All that unfolds is for my higher purpose as I am the next grand expression being revealed.
I let go of circumstances and judgments and simply look to thee. May I learn this time by triumph and not trial!
Thy will be done!

So it is. Amen!

December 9

Lord, I believe and trust You to develop in me: compassion, creativity, curiosity, confidence, courage, calm, connectedness, and clarity.

Your peace is deep within me, calling me to be in harmony with all. Lift from me the worry, thoughts, and judgments that keep me from experiencing and being the light You intended me to be. May all confusion fall to the clarity of owning, believing, and trusting in freedom, joy, harmony, and wholeness. So the complications in my mind are wanting to transition to this freedom of my spirit. The things that temporarily worry me fade to being at rest in all circumstances in faith, trust, and peace, as this is where Your victory rests in me. My human nature is to be and experience You, the divine.

Amen!

December 10

May I grow in learning to let go of that which I have no control. I strive to be available with my gifts and to bless all that is good and right revealed in Your light. I am not lost, confused, or frustrated, but instead, I know my mission is to encourage, nurture, and love.

May my reality be to trust and rest in the gleeful and continual unfolding of Your perfect plan. It's only as I see it incomplete that I fret, but I know that eventually, it will be completely revealed to me. So I wait and can contemplate Your glorious fête.

Amen.

December 11

May I know and feel that You hold me in the palm of Your hand.

May I surrender worry for trust in You.

May I cease to live in regret and live in the presence of Your healing.

I give up the "what ifs" for the "what is" in Your presence.

I rest upon Your promises. May this day unfold Your peace, presence, and grace in and through me.

Amen.

December 12

May my primary language be of the heart from the start.

All things are lessons from You to guide and lead me to Your light of eternal hope. May I shed the darkness from the night and focus on the peace of Your light.

Your love rests upon me and does not skip one heartbeat. May I grow to better understand the depth and intensity of Your love so it can fortify me.

Whatever is before me is a blessing or a lesson to bring eternal life. May I be free of emotions that cause me to cling to lesser things. What unfolds in this moment is the unwrapping of the gifts that uplift. As I open the eyes of my heart to who and what You have placed before me, I take a step closer to You.

Amen!

December: Trust

December 13

Last night, I was with my Dad when he breathed his last breath. In our youth, we gain insight into life's real purpose and death's transition. Losing Your father digs in earth's ground the same feeling of being lost in a park or a store as a child.

But in those childhood moments, You knew that someone who loved You was still near and would endlessly look for You. The death of an earthly father leaves You with the stunning reality that that feeling of protection is now only something You can give. At the same time, You can receive that comfort of protection from Your Heavenly Father.

You cannot compare differing experiences of Your loved one's earthly departures. I've said goodbye now to a father, mother, brother, and a son, all in God's call to each soul just as He will call mine. I've carried on from Reid and was left with a different path and purpose that He now guides. I've learned the truest kindness from the simple life of my father; he had no enemies, kept no score, was grateful for everything he had, and he never desired what he did not have. He worked hard, paid his bills, and loved his family and neighbors.

I have certainty that the Lord said to him last night, "Well done, good and faithful servant," in the company of my mom, brother, and son.

Amen.

_____
_____
_____
_____
_____

December 14

Compassion, understanding, and forgiveness . . . may this be the trilogy of the days yet to come.

May I develop the discipline to understand the reality I think I create. I want to naturally think of the love from You, this unity that destroys all hate. It's not too late; You have created me for this time right now.

All my fear dissolves like waves at the shoreline, inviting me to stand on solid ground. In this, the me I created falls before who You created me to be.

Amen.

December 15

Take from me the inability to accept what IS. Not fully acknowledging what You made me to be denies my authenticity.

It reluctantly creates the suffering that You never meant for me. Only through the confusion of delusion do I lose the freedom of spirit You gave me. Instead, I yearn to become totally free. As what IS . . . is what was meant to be.

My experience of pain was to grow me. But suffering is a choice that's up to me.

So release me from the frown I've let distract me from You. This suffering only exists in my mind. My stubborn thoughts will dissolve into a new reality so I can be just the way You created me to be!

Amen.

December 16

I can be strong and courageous as You are with me wherever I go.

I receive, appreciate, and accept what You lay before me. My mind desires the freedom to surrender its entanglements to see and experience You in me. That is my path to be free. My mind complicates and only survives, but my heart simplifies and enables me to thrive. The pointless busyness of everyday life is no longer for me. It's when I learn to surrender and just be that I find the deepest peace You meant for me.

Amen!

December 17

You are near to me as I call on You. I am at peace any moment I calm the mental stew with this truth of You. I realize You are the cure to any anxiety, but I need to remember to call on You.

As I focus my mind and surrender my heart, I feel Your calm within, for You are my anchor in any mental storm. I was born for this peace to be mine now and forevermore.

So call to me and remind me that when life's circumstances cause me trouble, Your stillness waits for me in Your protective bubble.

Amen.

December 18

Lord, may I see You with the simplicity of a child's eyes.
    I remember when I could dream without fear or hesitation. The awe and trust of how big You are banished the negative ideas in my young state of mind, where peace is the find. Make me fresh like I was new again, just learning how to be a best friend.
    That incredible rush is still available to me.
    I need to truly trust and start my first thoughts with Thee instead of me and not worry about what others might think. If I'm not careful, the worries that made my dreams blurry come back in a flurry. When I fixate on the problems, they are magnified, but when I surrender them to trust in You, I'm no longer blue with the mental flu.
    You have said many are the plans in the mind of a man, but it is the purpose of the LORD that will stand. That promise to trust and be takes me back to young me with gleeful passion.
    A change in my attitude gives me a great new latitude. I am trading my fear for trust!
    So Lord, stop me at the first thought that fails to see just how much You love me. I discover within me the child of my true humanity. It frees me to reflect the best of You and wait in this serenity.

Amen!

_____
_____
_____
_____
_____

December: Trust

December 19

Your call is constant, and Your comfort surrounds me. I run to You in my troubles. May I surrender to Your love as everything before me is in Your caring presence. I'm grateful for this truth and that hope, even though I'm often a dope. I can only become light from Your light of love. May my heart be opened, ready to receive Your offering.

I've learned that in You is my hope, and all that unfolds from You is filled with understanding. You are always waiting for me to see more clearly and walk more closely. You are fully present with me, as Your creation reminds me.

Only by leaning in and learning more of Your love is there freedom. Your love supplies and heals, carrying away negativity. May my dark emotions float through me like a vanishing cloud, and may they be silenced so they are no longer loud.

I am okay as I know I am adored and loved by You, who alone can cause the unspeakable to dissolve without a doubt! Forgive me when I cast doubt on Your love, thinking there's a limit when it's neverending. May my strength be renewed, my spirit united with You. Through Your love, I heal and carry on knowing You're my direct boss.

With the highs and lows beyond my control, my soul prepares for an eternity of peace with You. In the end, I cannot lose. I've arrived and am waiting for that final lifting from Your call.

Amen!

_____
_____
_____

December 20

My Lord, God of love, power, and majesty, overseer of all, may I see with the clarity You call me to. When my mind is fixated on You, I look up to see only the possibilities. But when I'm lost in lesser things, and I forget to surrender it all to You, I believe it's up to me. I'm lost in the dust and the rust, but in the valley, I look up, and there You are, calling my name and telling me no one's to blame. Anything not worthy of You has gone up in flames.

You bring me to the shore, where You restore all that you created for me to be free and full of Your light and love. My God, my savior, my friend and neighbor, You haven't taken Your eye off me from the moment You picked me to be Yours.

Thank You, God, as I draw near and trust how dear I am to You! For I AM a child of God!

Amen!

December 21

May I be strong, and may my heart take courage as I wait for the LORD!

I wait on Him in struggle. I wait on Him in celebration. I wait on Him on the long journey in the midst of life's fight, even surrounded by blight. But I keep imagining Heaven's in sight. As I see the bright light that is evidence of His might, I wait to experience His full delight.

My Lord lures me, calling my very own name. It matters not what challenge is before me, be it high or way down low, as it cannot shake this feeling that, ultimately, I am His beloved in whom He is well pleased! So why take fright in any old night? Instead, soak in His delight. Even though I can get really down and frown, I always return to the promise of just whose I am. For the Lord is my perpetual friend, who never stops talking to me, all the way to the end and beginning again!

Amen!

December 22

Lord, it's easy to say, "Worry about nothing and pray about everything." But Lord, help me let go of the fuss and learn to deeply lean into trust.

My instinct is to first rely on myself, but Your word instructs me to replace this habit with the faith to see what You've already done. Only then can I truly see the depth of everything You've put in place uniquely for me. My heart knows Your plans are beyond human hands as You call me to trust and follow thee. When I lean into Your call of peace, trust, and surrender, I see the past problems I put in front of Your Heavenly plans.

Our world seems in constant chaos and confusion, but I know deep in my soul that it's always Your will that grows and paves the road to Heavenly heights, which I will ultimately know. I'll learn more in this time and place to have peace from beyond outer space. You are stretching me to believe what I cannot yet see.

Your plans are good, and I call out to You to guide my steps by believing and just truly trusting You.

Amen.

December 23

I give up on being lost in thought in all ways. I do not need to attempt control, for You have written the script! Since darkness is just an absence of light, let me embrace Your light. Worries melt in gratitude.

Love cleanses fear and enables me to be free in my being. It's a mindset of surrender.

The condition of my heart is what determines my mindset, so I meditate and pray to my creator and protector each day.

When I turn to You, my fight disappears with my blight, and I focus solely on Your Heavenly prize. All I had to do was simply rest and trust in You.

Amen!

December 24

Trusting in Your grace, my human form reflects Your divine light.
    Your love for me cannot be reduced in my darkest hour. My flaws and imperfections make me who I am. Your love for me knows no bounds. You are my strength and my source. I use the gifts You gave me to be a unique expression of Your likeness. The kindness I speak of is the leak of the power of Your spirit.
    As I am true to myself, I am able to be who You created to make You proud. Just as You will say upon my return to the Heavenly, "In You, I am well pleased." Your loving parent's heart overflows with love and pride because of my earthly ride.
    You never leave me, always accept me, and endlessly call me Your child, for that is what I am.
    I'm not the judgment of others but the value You created me to be. You guide my every move, sliding me Heaven-bound. Indeed, You know what You're doing. I eradicate shame and blame; instead, Your endless flame is the one true game as You call me by name.

Amen!

_____
_____
_____
_____
_____

December 25

Lord, may I trust in You beyond that which I do. This is the trust that will allow fear to melt into courage.
Trust that makes defeat dance for delight through anything.
Trust that takes emotions through the storm cleansed to become my greatest delight.
Trust that the day of boredom is storing needed energy to experience eternal euphoria.
Trust that the gym of life is for the beach shores of Heaven.
No tears will have been wasted, no challenge far from You. You were knowing and loving me the whole darn time.
I just need to get where You are through developing my muscle of trust. Surrendering in You is trusting in You! But I haven't earned it. I don't deserve it! Then I hear Your whisper that I am enough just the way I was meant to be, and You know all I did as it was to cure my sight to see I am enough because I am Yours. You see my trust is in You, as that's who I was meant to be: YOURS! When I met the truth of trust, You were just waiting for me to stop doing it on my own, waiting on me to JUST TRUST and BE!

Amen!

_____
_____
_____
_____
_____

December 26

May my kindness be a way of life, not a strategy. May Your spirit create in me a clean heart and genuineness that is free to be transparent. What I once saw in others as naive, I now believe. It's easy to trust You as I must, which defies the lust to shield and protect myself and believe that others are out to get me.

In this new paradigm, I can now rhyme in the rhythm of time. As I experience the sublime in real time, I trust, receive, and am confident that You protect me.

So because of the three of the trinity, I can rest and be at peace through all of life's unexpectancies.

That is the peace that surpasses all understanding.

Amen!

December: Trust

December 27

When ego was my outer coating, the Lord was not seen within me. As I shed this egoic coating of mine, the radiant light of the Lord now can be seen.

What is the difference between thriving and surviving through life? Thriving is living in the spirit, while surviving is living from the ego. It's the Struggle in life that allows the transition from surviving to thriving. The pain of the world feeds the evolution that fuels the medicine, creating the understanding of the absolute need of the Lord. The spirit blooms the languages of love out of living truthfully and authentically. I am now devoid of the ego's stage creations to appease man, creating false realities and depriving us of God's oxygen of life.

His truths sustain steadfast Love, which ultimately wins in God's grace!

Amen!

December 28

Lord, my heart is not troubled, for my faith is in You!
My hope, God, is not broken because it is strengthened by You!
My anger subsides and gives way to the light of truth for You to make things clear and new.
I struggle, Father, only when I forget and withhold the outstretching of my arms to You.
My Trust is in You, Lord. My hope washes away all fears and illusions. In You, I see eternity. I see the explanations to the uncertainties, mysteries, and misunderstandings of man.
I no longer live in wonder as all confusion awaits the appointed moment that unveils Your perfect love, truth, and eternal comfort, specifically awaiting me in total trust of Your goodness for me!
Wow, You really are an amazing God!
Of course, I believe in You. You believed in me from the second You created me!

Amen!

December 29

I am filled with the precious fullness that comes from the Lord.
My anxiousness dissolves in my Trust in God.

No fear lasts within me but is merely a cloud of passing emotion whose gray turns to blue in the light of the spirit.

When my vision goes from the depths to the heights, it sees the cheer, joy, and love around me.

I am in unity as I delight in the harmony among us, free from the competition of separation, as I embrace the wholeness of the Father, Spirit, and Son, from whom my hope comes. The spirit of the souls that surround me lifts me to heights where only Heaven is known.

Amen!

December 30

Dear God, Your word in Isaiah 43:2 (ESV) tells us, "When You pass through the waters, I will be with You; and through the rivers, they shall not overwhelm You; when You walk through fire, You shall not be burned, and the flame shall not consume You."

Then why does my weakness prevent me from trusting You more than the man-made life preserver. I walk through the fires of life with fear.

May Your truth and reality reign in me, compelling me with the strength and power of Your promises.

Melt that which allows my mind to be lost in falsely believing in the separation of Your promises, as they are truly for me!

May the fires of life be extinguished by Your Love that lights the path of my feet for eternity.

Truth, trust, and love; anything less is not of You.

Amen!

December 31

May I love my neighbor just as they are, not by how I think they should be from afar. We each are different by Your unique design.

The rose does not look at the lilac with envy, but it's satisfied to grow with the sun's ray with its own fragrance on display.

May I see Your miracles at work and be free to be all You're calling me to be.

If only I could erase the desire in my mind's inner mire. When I run the race with Your grace, I'm not looking at the face next to me. My eyes glow from my heart's flow as I go . . . go . . . go!

As You've put me in my own lane and called for me to plant my eyes upon You, I leave the worry to You about how others do.

I know I'm through with the race when the sun of grace puts a permanent smile on my face.

Amen!

About REID Foundation

The REID Foundation is a 501 (c)(3) nonprofit organization dedicated to utilizing the healing power of music, creative expression, and other therapeutic modalities to bring "front-line therapy" and prevention to communities and those impacted by the opioid crisis, substance abuse, mental health issues or life crisis.

The REID Foundation was founded by Rex Elsass, Chairman of The Strategy Group Co., who lost his son Reid Elsass to addiction on June 2, 2019. Reid's love of music and creative expression sparked the Foundation's movement to create innovative and life-changing programs to scale worldwide.

Our mission is to
REACH EVERYONE IN DISTRESS
with the healing power of music and creative expression and promote research for the healing of trauma through emerging therapies.

Scan QR code to support

Reid.Foundation

THIS BOOK IS PROTECTED INTELLECTUAL PROPERTY

The author of this book values Intellectual Property. The book you just read is protected by Instant IP™, a proprietary process, which integrates blockchain technology giving Intellectual Property "Global Protection." By creating a "Time-Stamped" smart contract that can never be tampered with or changed, we establish "First Use" that tracks back to the author.

Instant IP™ functions much like a Pre-Patent™ since it provides an immutable "First Use" of the Intellectual Property. This is achieved through our proprietary process of leveraging blockchain technology and smart contracts. As a result, proving "First Use" is simple through a global and verifiable smart contract. By protecting intellectual property with blockchain technology and smart contracts, we establish a "First to File" event.

Protected by Instant IP™

LEARN MORE AT INSTANTIP.TODAY

www.ingramcontent.com/pod-product-compliance
Lightning Source LLC
Chambersburg PA
CBHW052130070526
44585CB00017B/1770